Mousy Cats and Sheepish Coyotes

Mousy Cats and Sheepish Coyotes

THE SCIENCE OF ANIMAL PERSONALITIES

John A. Shivik

Beacon Press
Boston

BEACON PRESS
Boston, Massachusetts
www.beacon.org

Beacon Press books
are published under the auspices of
the Unitarian Universalist Association of Congregations.

20 19 18 17   8 7 6 5 4 3 2 1

This book is printed on acid-free paper that meets the uncoated paper
ANSI/NISO specifications for permanence as revised in 1992.

Text design and composition by Kim Arney

Library of Congress Cataloging-in-Publication Data

Names: Shivik, John A., author.
Title: Mousy cats and sheepish coyotes : the science of animal personalities
    / John A. Shivik, PhD.
Description: Boston : Beacon Press, 2017. | Includes bibliographical
    references and index.
Identifiers: LCCN 2017011322 (print) | LCCN 2017034030 (e-book) |
    ISBN 9780807071526 (e-book) | ISBN 9780807071519 (hardcover : alk. paper)
Subjects: LCSH: Animal psychology. | Animal behavior. | Human-animal
    relationships.
Classification: LCC QL785 (e-book) | LCC QL785 .S472 2017 (print) |
    DDC 591.5—dc23
LC record available at https://lccn.loc.gov/2017011322

For Roberta and John Shivik Sr.,
who created the clan of individuals: Teresa, JoAnne,
Elizabeth, Michael, David, and myself

*Always remember that
you are absolutely unique,
just like everyone else.*

— MARGARET MEAD

Contents

My Cat and Dogma

My cat, for all practical purposes, is an asshole.

To his credit, he had a bit of an uphill battle with me, and my opinion may not be entirely his fault. I have never been one to like cats. At an intellectual level, it doesn't make sense to bond with them. Compared to loyal and obsequious dogs, cats are so independent. Aloof. Sneaky. Selfish. Sanctimonious, even. They're little bastards that don't care about you or anyone else, or if they do, they want it only on their own terms. Completely conditional love. They expect, they demand. Finicky? Are you kidding me? *I* didn't get to choose my meals as a kid.

It is trite to write that cats are the counterpoint to dogs. It is a truism to conclude that there are dog people and cat people. But I'll note, if you haven't figured this out already, that I grew up a dog person.

And then there is Pingüino.

Pingüino has been the herald of my triumphs as a father, the narrator of the death of my marriage. He has been the one annoying companion that has been with me through it all. He has tested the limits of his nine lives. An obnoxious vocalizer, his needy meow is tuned to the tone and key of fingernails on a chalkboard. He is a black and white tuxedo cat who was insensitively bequeathed to me while I was in my old life, when I often traveled to Spain.

He wasn't my chosen pet but rather the result of passive-aggressive miscommunication between my erstwhile wife and me. A confidant of hers at the time was moving, so it seemed the perfect solution for him and gift for me: a loud cat for a dog person. I was away on one of my work trips to España, so perhaps it was more about noncommunication than miscommunication, but the indisputable fact was that a new, young cat was in the house. I arrived home jet-lagged, and he greeted me by attacking my toes.

"Merrrrrreow," he said, haughtily.

Pingüino's body is a portrait of inconsistency. Sitting, his haunches ooze to either side of his hips, and his butt is an order of magnitude larger than his head. He has the shape of an overweight penguin, pelage divided between no color and all colors at once—hence his name. He has both eyebrows, left and right, but the left is white and the right black. Against the sleekness of his fur, the long black hairs are invisible, and only the white ones show, so he appears as if he has only one eyebrow. He's fat, loud, and lopsided. But he doesn't give a damn. Worse, he stares at me, judging, as if *I* look funny.

The cat has been with me for a decade now. He made the move from Logan, Utah, to Bishop, California, in 2010. There, he became a great killer of lizards and taunter of coyotes. The lord and master of the little mining-town shack where I lived with my family, Pingüino was hell on the smaller species of wildlife in our dilapidated subdivision. As a wildlife biologist, I cringed as he rained death upon the birds and reptiles. The Wildlife Society position statement on free-range and feral cats is clear: "Domestic cats have tremendous impacts on wildlife and are responsible for the extinction of numerous mammals, reptiles, and at least 33 bird species globally."[1] Professional societies deplore the wanton destruction caused by domestic cats. Pingüino was fixed and not feral, but he was an indoor-outdoor cat, and had a penchant for hunting in spite of—or adding to—his size. I installed bird feeders to supplement the local population and to assuage my guilt. The lizards did deliver some element of revenge, dulling his coat and slowing his progress by giving him parasitic worms, but the veterinarians sorted that out before we moved to Nevada City, California, after nine months in the Bishop hovel.

Pingüino was housed temporarily with my former sister-in-law while we moved to Nevada City. He rejected the kindness of his benefactor and escaped from her palatial horse-property rambler on the outskirts of Los Angeles. As most cat owners likely know, drastic change can be particularly hard on cats, and Pingüino acted out by making a break for it: he disappeared into the dry hills. Weeks after his escape, we were newly ensconced in a Nevada City rental five hundred miles away. We were certain that he was dead, a meal for the coyotes. Or so I thought when the phone rang. His Los Angeles chaperone was holding him near the phone.

"Meow," he said, the annoying voice unmistakable. Pingüino had cashed in a good two-thirds of his nine lives, but he was back, and a little put out by it. He seemed more annoyed to be submitting to domestication than about nearly losing his skin, but he incorporated the positives of Meow Mix and safety into his calculation and decided to come back. It was on his terms, after all.

The experiment of moving to Nevada City was a failure for our family too, and we had to leave there as well. On the verge of another move, I began to feel some sympathy for this cat. Cats are well known for being traumatized by change. Dogs are generally fine with moving from place to place, as long as they have you, their social group, with them. Cats require their *stuff*. When one moves a cat, it is best to not pack everything in the moving van but rather to bring familiar objects. Pooky the stuffed bear. A favorite rug or two ought to be brought along so that upon arriving in the new abode, the cat has an immediate sense of familiarity to soften the transition.

It was the third move in as many years. This time, however, only my son and I were headed back to our old house, the family unit torn asunder. Ostensibly for his benefit, I offered to bring Pingüino back to his familiar surroundings in Logan, Utah. There was no denying it anymore. The cat and I were a team.

In the time we were gone, other cats had discovered the Utah house's pet door. Upon our return they made use of it to invade and rudely steal Pingüino's food. I could tell when they came in, because Pingüino retreated to the tops of the kitchen cabinets and hid until I returned. Then, he'd voice his displeasure about the intruder to me. After a long day of work, his stentorian tones jangled my nerves.

I pointed out to him that it was his house. I do the human side and keep out the human robbers; he's responsible for the feline interlopers. He jumped down, meowed at me, and paced back and forth on the stairs so that I would lead the way to the second floor bathroom. He leapt in front of my feet and tripped me as I started toward the first step. He waited in the hall while I confirmed that the coast was clear and refilled his bowl. He would go in only after I did, but then, famished, he'd bury his face in the food. He has the ability to crunch cat kibble and to meow simultaneously. I've never heard anything like it before. It is the only time he sounds cute.

In the evenings now, when he is tired or just bored, he'll follow me to bed. His arrival on the mattress is unmistakable. Shaped like a bowling pin, he lands like a bowling ball. If I am sufficiently aware, I am able to guard my groin before he steps heavily on my crotch. He may stare at my face and engage a purr that reverberates in the room. He'll drop beside me, leaning in, and it sounds and feels as if I am being cuddled by a cement mixer.

I am still not a cat person, but I find myself drawn to and enamored with the guy. His characteristics are annoying, but they are also rather harmless in the grand scheme of things. More important, they provide countless stories, anecdotes unusual enough to qualify as comedy.

I understand why cats are often considered self-righteous, independent beasts. But Pingüino isn't any cat. He's a unique individual. I know him and realize that he is loving and emotional and dependent too, but in his own way. He speaks a singular and confusing language, but he does communicate his unique view of the world. He is absolutely distraught if I leave the house for more than a day and will follow me around and meow constantly upon my return after even a short business trip. His other behavioral proclivities may be familiar to those with similar feline entanglements too: he will lounge upon the desk as I write, then make a few laps back and forth over the keyboard until I shoo him away to fix his typos. The thing I find intriguing is the variety of surprising things he does that make him who he is—different from any other cat. Just now, he has squeezed to sit in a flowerpot on the windowsill beside me; folds of his butt overflow the rim like the top of a muffin. His tail crowds around the miniature lemon tree in the pot and his back presses its flowers away from the window so that he can observe the world from a slightly higher perch. He is ludicrous from the shoulders down, but his face betrays no discomfort or hint of diffidence. He glares superciliously upon the magpies hopping across the lawn.

Pingüino hasn't taught me to like all cats, but he has shown me how to notice and bond with a particular one. And what I like about him is that he's not a quiet objet d'art. Rather, I like him because of his difficulty—because of his personality.

Indeed, over time Pingüino bowled me over with his strength of personality. He is confident in knowing what he wants, isn't afraid to communicate it, and isn't overly self-conscious about striving forward, even if he looks silly or fails in his attempt. He's not the perfect, obedient dog of my dreams, but he's the exact companion I needed at the time. The little bastard has taught me the difference between what I think I want and what I actually need. I can't think of my home without him anymore, and the reason is not because he's a cat, but because he's *Pingüino*.

One might think that the idea of a book about individual animals' expressing themselves is, well, *duh*. So much is already known about their internal workings, especially the charismatic ones such as wolves, elephants, and whales.[2] Although it is far from universally accepted, the notion that animals, especially mammals, have emotional lives is not new.[3] A long line of authors have explored the subject, such as Masson and McCarthy's groundbreaking work in the 1980s; or Cynthia Moss discussing empathy in elephants, including describing how they use grieving and mourning rituals; or G. A. Bradshaw, who noted similarities between humans and animals when she documented elephant susceptibility to post traumatic stress.[4] Research showing that chimpanzees empathize like humans and that bonobos are adept at peacefully resolving conflicts has been widely publicized.[5] Especially for those species that have long been considered big brained or advanced, it is nothing new to say that animals have emotional lives. Even Darwin was comfortable comparing humans with the chimps and apes as he pointed out that "some of the expressive actions of monkeys are interesting . . . namely from being closely analogous to those of man."[6]

My purpose in this book is not to reexamine a fait accompli, preaching something that many people already know through either intuition or the works of previous authors: animals have emotions and intelligence. The point of this book is to embark from the knowledge that certain species think and feel and to explore what individuality means to humans, to the panoply of species on earth, and to our relationship with them.

Animal intelligence and emotion have broader implications. First, I won't settle for the notion that animals all feel in the same way. Different animals, even those in the same species, are more complicated than that; their emotional responses, their *personalities* differ. This book draws on research and stories from my life with my animal companions, but I also draw on my vocation as a wild-life biologist to show that, like Pingüino, an animal of *any* species is unique, with an individual personality. Those particular personalities—theirs and ours—are what drives the bonds between us. Second, as a scientist I can't stop with just accepting that animals have personalities; instead, I'm compelled to investigate why they do. Finally, I can roam through familiar territory, telling stories about cats and elephants and primates, but let's push further into unlikely places too. For example, what about beings as alien to humans as the dinosaurs and their modern-day descendants?

Feeling like I was being watched, I put down the dishes and turned away from the sink. Highlighted and backlit by the deck, a bird darkened the door. She took a step in. Wesley the chicken cooed inquisitively, cocking her head and turning broadside to me.

"You're kidding me," I thought.

Lipless and toothless, domestic chickens lack the ability to smile, but they do express themselves. They make soothing sounds, gentle clucks and coos like high, soft purrs. Wesley was a Plymouth Rock hen, barred black and white with a regal comb and wattles. She was a puff ball of a butterball and was standing between me and my outdoor deck.

"Shoo," I said, and she strutted out slowly. "Down. Out." I corralled her down the stairs and into the lush yard. Chickens should dig bugs from the yard, I thought, not beg scraps from the sink.

Wesley is different from the other chickens, but it can be difficult to describe the differences using concise and objective language.

Humans aren't even experts at reading and describing signals among our own species. If we were, there wouldn't be such an overwhelming need for advice columns and couples therapy. We use our own experience to guess at others' motivations and are ironically flabbergasted when we've mistaken our partner's intentions. Now, it is my charge to explain the motivations of a chicken, and in the rest of the book it is going to get much harder as I try to understand the personalities of animals we humans think have even less in common with us.

On some days I consider Wesley to be a bold chicken. That is, she'll come up onto my house's deck and explore. The other chickens remain in the safety of familiar haunts at the other side of the yard, eyeing my vegetable garden. She seems to think ahead and to focus on the opportunity to find new morsels for herself. The deck and kitchen are new environments—completely uncontested and without competition from the other birds. Being there alone, she can claim the scraps of all things dropped during meals and cocktail parties. But is it a bold thing to do, to walk into the kitchen as I am finishing cleaning after a meal? I'd never harmed her before. Indeed, I am the obvious provider of food and water. Perhaps she isn't so bold but rather curious and smart.

Then again, as she has seen that I am the one who has brought pellets and scraps to the coop so many times before, could it be possible that Wesley has other motivations? Could she, like my mother, communicate love through food? Could she be showing affection, strutting through the kitchen door clucking and cooing, only to have me, misreading the cues, shoo her away? I doubt it, but I will never truly know.

But her exact motivation isn't the only point. It is also that behaviorally she is in such contrast to the others in the flock. Phyllis, an extravagantly coifed Polish chicken, is not so bright as Wesley. Phyllis is the shy one among the troop of backyard hens. When the others would retreat inside on cold winter nights, she'd often sit alone, outside, under the eaves of the coop, where icicles dripped drops upon her. It was difficult to determine whether or not freezing rain made it through the massive bubble of her head feathers, but it certainly did not look comfortable. She looked confused, but remained calm when I gently picked her up to put her in the coop. She wasn't afraid. Was she dumb because she didn't realize that in the summer her shaded perch was excellent, but could not fathom the contextual notion that in winter it was a dreadful spot? Was she bold because she calmly let me pick her up?

Words such as *shy* or *bold* or *smart* or *dumb* can fail us. In a different context, Phyllis is the most shy; when the other chickens, led by Wesley, boldly move forward into new hunting grounds, she moves so reluctantly. She is satisfied with the familiar pellets in the coop. She keeps to the same perch. She doesn't appear to have the lust for adventure that Wesley has.

What are the right words to describe this behavior? I can only infer. Is one who does not seek adventure and the excitement of new things shy and weak or are there other, more appropriate interpretations? Could it be that Phyllis stays at home because she has achieved Zen? Does she live in the moment, completely content? Have I mislabeled her as the slow and dumb one, as if I were calling the Buddha a stodgy homebody?

And what about an expectation that only the animals most like us, mammals, are most likely to have personalities? If chickens can be unique, every one of them, many other species can be too.

The stories of individual animals and their personalities have been literally pecking at my door for years. They have been both joyful and intensely sad, which created a nagging conflict within me. I've fancied myself a scientist, and so in my scientific writings, I rejected overt study of animals as emotional and intelligent individuals.

There have been many reasons why I have not and could not have written on the subject of animal personality previously. If nothing else, I would not have wanted to appear soft in the rough and tumble world of scientific cliques. But why would the study of animal personalities cause consternation among the scientific elite? There are a few reasons, but the first is dogma. We scientists have a long history of resisting change in thought. The second, which is a result of the first, is a lack of scientific foundation. Things are changing, however, and researchers are entering a newly enlightened age where there is a creeping desire to peer into the individual lives of animals: to understand them as intelligent and emotional beings and to study the evolutionary reasons for being the individuals they are.

———

How did I fall, and rest, in the pit of scientific limitation, eyes closed to so many of the complexities and wonders of individual animal behavior? It started with school, where I was taught, above all, the dangers of anthropomorphizing. The word *anthropomorphize* is from the Greek for "human form," and it originally came into existence as a way to describe the ancient gods, which were so humanlike in their actions. Eventually it was extended to describe animals when they were humanlike too. My training was like the 1980s juvenile-justice attempt at "scared straight," and under the thinking of the gatekeepers of my field, admitting that animals have human characteristics was the gateway drug to the opiate of subjectivity and scientific ruin.

Although it's not widely known now, early, prominent biologists once accepted phenomena such as inner states and emotions in animals as early as 1872, when Charles Darwin embraced the notion in *The Expression of the Emotions in Man and Animals*.[7] Darwin is a household name for the theory of evolution, but certainly not for theories about animal emotion. Why? Why did some of his musings make such a profound impression, but his thoughts on the evolutionary pressures that created animal emotion and personality sink into obscurity? Darwin used anecdotes to argue that similar physiologies in humans and other animals must indicate similar internal feelings. By contracting the same musculature that humans do, monkeys are expressing pleasure, joy, and affection or grief, disappointment, astonishment, and terror. Anger is one that was particularly obvious, as Darwin observed, "Monkeys also redden from passion" the way anger blushes a human face.

Standing on Darwin's metaphoric shoulders, George John Romanes inferred that even species very unlike humans have humanlike internal attributes.[8] Worms, he surmised, feel surprise and fear. Insects have curiosity. Fish can play or be jealous or angry. Reptiles are affectionate, and birds can be prideful or experience terror. Mammals, of course, exhibit all the emotions above, plus hate, cruelty, and shame. If different animals have subtle but evolutionarily important differences in such emotions, they have different levels of passions and intelligence. Individuals would have different personalities that natural selection acts upon. Romanes, writing a book entitled *Animal Intelligence*, was too much for Victorian England, however.

While Romanes, Darwin, and many of their contemporaries would have confessed that humans can't see into the mind or interpret the language of a cat's or chicken's mental circuitry, the squishiness of their speculative science generated a vigorous backlash in the form of a zealous quest for complete objectivity. Rather than run the risk of overinterpreting behaviors, C. Lloyd Morgan pontificated the black and white, dogmatic, "correct" method of behavioral science that came to be known as Morgan's Canon. It set back the study of animal personality by one hundred years.

The Canon is fleshed out in Morgan's tome on comparative psychology where he increasingly demands a certain discipline of behavioral analysis.[9] Morgan insists that animal behaviors not be described in terms of anthropomorphic or higher psychic activity such as love, gentleness, deceit, and so forth, but instead be interpreted only by the simplest, observable, mechanisms. Precisely, he wrote, "in no case may we interpret an action as the outcome of the exercise of a higher physical faculty if it can be interpreted as the outcome of the exercise of one which stands lower in the psychological scale."[10] It is the animal behaviorist's adaptation of the golden rule of parsimony in science: Occam's razor, the idea that the simplest explanation is always the best. Not inferring that an animal has internal emotions or ambitions, one assumes, is simpler than inferring that it has them. Biologists recognized differences in individual behavior, sometimes, but they struggled to accept the existence of personality and dodged the word, trying to force the concept into terms such as *behavioral syndromes, coping styles, animal temperament*, and *interindividual variation*. Certain contortions are needed to arrive at the supposed Morganic objectivity. Occam's razor has been used like a chainsaw slicing at the trees, oblivious to the forest.

Professors instilled the Canon through catechism, and as a young scientist I was susceptible to the brainwashing. My prime directive was to eschew anthropomorphic interpretations such as animal personality. "In no case may we interpret an action as the outcome of the exercise of a higher physical faculty."[11] In my undergraduate textbook on animal behavior the authors adopted a supercilious tone as they hailed, "C. Lloyd Morgan helped stop the anecdotal tradition, thereby helping send comparative psychology toward the objective science it is today."[12] Thus spoke Saint Morgan. Amen. Under that inculcation, my rejection of anthropomorphism grew into haughty disdain. Any slip into using human thoughts or feelings to help understand animals was a cardinal sin. As a young scientist, I ridiculed people for it: I would judge as unscientific, wishy-washy, and subjective sentimentalists those who said an animal had feelings or personality.

———

I was also taught that I had to essentially prove objectivity by reducing behavior to mathematical equations. Biologists, suffering from "physics envy," sought to prove how scientific biology was by reducing it to math. Only if you could model it with an equation was it real. Animals were numbers, not named individuals. Individual variation was a nuisance and its source was thought to be undefinable because "in no case may we interpret an action as the outcome of the exercise of a higher physical faculty." Ironically, physicists were comfortable enough to name quarks quirky names such as *strange* and *charm*. But biologists had to work overtime to prove their objective bona fides.

The simplest and most relied on statistical techniques in biology use the mathematic mean, the average, and the variability of the population around that average. It requires lumping measurements of individuals into groups to devise accurate descriptors. For example, adult males in the United States currently average 195 pounds, and females weigh, on average, 166 pounds.[13]

Why can statistics such as these be a problem? First, almost no one is average. Most adult females weigh between 111 and 251 pounds and males between 136 and 274 pounds, but it is rare to find a female who weighs exactly 166 or a male who weighs precisely 195. Indeed, the probability of selecting a male within the population that weighs between 194 ½ pounds and 195 ½ pounds is only 0.009.[14] Fewer than one person in one hundred is of average weight. So, if describing individual humans, what good is the average if not even one out of one hundred actually weighs that amount? And weight is only one factor. There is variation in height, hair color, skin color, behavior . . .

As the pioneering scientist Rebecca Fox eloquently put it, "Individual differences in behavior were long ignored as 'noise' around an adaptive mean."[15] Trained as a wildlife biologist, I find it rather amazing that the focus of my scientific world, for statistical convenience, has been the biologically inappropriate thing. Sameness doesn't drive nature, differences do. It's not only the average that is interesting but also the differences among individuals. The math may allow researchers to calculate an average, but knowing just a little about elephants, chickens, or my cat proves otherwise: there is no such thing as an average person or animal. The haze from which I have recently awakened is that the "lack of knowledge about the proximate mechanisms of individual differences is due in large part to a focus on population means in both behavioral and physiological research."[16]

But there was more in the training from which I, and many others, need to recover. Trains of Morgans chugged inexorably down a narrow track, stuck to rails of constrained thinking, a world devoid of diversity. There was the fallacy of the name, for instance. In a blind haste to appear objective, scientists bathe in numbers instead of acknowledging the individual. I should have paid more attention to Shakespeare in my youth. Juliet Capulet's musing about Romeo Montague should have been a clue. The act of the name, and not its spelling, is the importance and essence of the argument. A name, whether it is Wolf 832F or Rose, immediately identifies the animal as unique among all others.

There was the fallacy of human exceptionalism. With other animals, especially other mammals with such similar internal circuitry as our own, is it appropriate to infer internal state based on external activity? Given the equivalent physiologies of diverse species, it is actually simpler to infer that animals have motivations and are driven by emotion than it is to deny the existence of their firing neurons. Frans de Waal asserts: "If two closely related species act the same under similar circumstances, the mental processes behind their behavior are likely the same too."[17] I can't ask Pingüino if he's satisfied, but his calm demeanor and purr give it away.

There was more, a reductionism of behavior to absurdity, the idea that because sometimes individuals act exactly the same, they all actually were the same. Stimulus, response. As if a rap on my patellar tendon, which causes a reflexive kick, is proof that I am no different from another person with the same reflex. There are more complicated examples too: fixed action patterns. These behaviors are like elaborate reflexes, and the textbook example is of the graylag goose retrieving an errant egg.[18] If an egg rolls away from a nesting goose, her response is choreographed, automatic, and identical among all her kind. She stretches her neck forward and scoops her bill back along the ground using a side to side swing, bringing the egg back into her nest. The amusing thing is that the behavior has an all or nothing aspect: once she stretches her neck, the dance isn't about the egg anymore. A mischievous scientist can take the rolled-out egg away after her bill swinging has started, and she will continue to swing and scoop as if the egg were still there. In the jargon, the rolled-out egg is a releaser, as if the scooping behavior is stored up inside the animal, waiting for the signal to let it out.

Given such examples, early ethologists argued that animals are preprogrammed machines, automatic, dumb. The thought was that if scientists just knew all the details, the releasers and rewards for everything, we could fully understand all behavior. By skimming Occam's razor down to the skin, we could explain all behavior as, first, a genetically programmed initial response to a stimulus and, second, a response that is sometimes shaped through encouragement by reward or discouragement by a negative result. Stimulus, response, reward changes to stimulus, greater response. Stimulus, response, pain becomes stimulus, less response. It is the essence of what is known as operant conditioning, or learning through trial and error. Animal behavior reduced to Java script.

Given the diversity of the animals around us, perhaps the reductionism seems impossible to embrace, but the notion of animals as preprogrammed machines still exists in ivory towers. Not long ago I had an academic colleague emphatically assert that behavior is nothing but "the result of its consequences." He is a fundamentalist, a result of the reasoning of B. F. Skinner, who perhaps best expressed his viewpoint in a conversation with Temple Grandin. When

Grandin observed how it would be great to know more about the brain, Skinner reportedly responded, "We don't need to learn about the brain, we have operant conditioning."[19] Skinner's contribution to our understanding of learning was groundbreaking and his impact on the science was phenomenal, but the vehemence of his intellectual descendants was a double-edged sword that set science back by generations. Their conclusions were guarded with religious fervor.

A trained acolyte of the church of objective behaviorism, I was stuck within a closed cell, not able to admit that animals could have internal emotional states. That prevented any possibility of achieving the next important step. If all animals were programmable units, and numbers at that, the idea of variance between them was a nuisance, and not the most important aspect of their behavior. I had to discover, first through observation and then through unlearning the dogma I had encountered in my training, that the importance of animal behavior was not only in how it came to be but also in how it differed between individuals.

The first cracks in the wall came when my belief about using tools came into question.

As humans, we repeatedly attempt to find some unique thing we do that other animals do not. But we risk overstating the importance of what we do well and fail to acknowledge the significance of what other animals can achieve given their unique skills and abilities. We point out the limits for other animals due to physiology—such as lacking opposable thumbs—but ignore how their behaviors overcome physical limitations. Thus, it is not only in religious circles that we conclude that humans are different, very special animals. We do it in many secular ways too.

Even before I became a biologist, for example, I was aware of the common refrain that *Homo sapiens* was different because we are the only species that uses tools. Scientists and laypersons alike, molded by the same anthropocentric zeitgeist, were tempted to hold fast to human superiority. And this was in spite of K. R. L. Hall and George Schaller writing, even before I was born, a little note about how individual otters choose certain rocks for certain tasks.[20] Some deference was given to apes, being so close to us, and that is where tool-use research has progressed most. By the time I began my studies, however, my eyes were opened to wider possibilities. I found that chimpanzees, orangutans, and bonobos not only use tools but they will work through multiple tool choices for complex problems: they choose the correct short tool to use to get to the correct long tool they need to get to food. Completely nonsimian New Caledonian crows, famous for being dexterous tool users, will also use a series of separate tools sequentially.[21] They don't even have hands.

Indeed, animals use tools on the ground and in the trees and in the air. Even in the oceans. By 2005 researchers were looking in what would have been thought the most unlikely places: diving in Shark Bay, off Western Australia, researchers noticed that wild dolphins search the sea floor for sponges. Finding the right one, the dolphins use sponges as tools to probe the substrate for fish.[22] The dogma of tool use was another example of poor science, assuming the absence of proof as proof of absence. Humans and many nonhuman animals most definitely use tools. So that does not set us humans apart.

Further dogmatic "proof" of human uniqueness were observations about another aspect of the human condition: lateralization. That is, handedness. About 90 percent of humans are right-handed.[23] Are we unique because of this? Why did it take until 2011 for Bill Hopkins and his collaborators to investigate our next of kin, chimpanzees, and when they examined more than seven hundred chimpanzees living in four different places, they determined that the little apes are mostly (60–70 percent) right-handed too.[24] Other labs replicated studies in other places outside the United States, and indeed, they confirmed hand bias in chimps, from Zambia to Spain.[25] Common marmosets prefer using one hand over the other, but one would never know from looking at the average; the species has equal numbers of lefties and righties.[26] Primates, so much like humans, are often given a pass, but if we look beyond, we see species as different from ourselves as marsupials favor one hand over the other; red kangaroos, rednecked wallabies, eastern grey kangaroos, and brush-tailed bettongs, resting tripedal on legs and tail, are overwhelmingly left-handed.[27] Even North American elk prefer a certain foot.[28]

Not only were advances in scientific research opening my eyes to the drawbacks of our human-centered worldview. Another crack occurred when my dog, Gretchen, helped me see how human hubris and our desire to set ourselves apart from the other animals can cloud our thinking. Recently I heard the famous journalist and author of *Natural Born Heroes*, Christopher McDougall, give an interview on KUER's *RadioWest* in which he drew a sharp distinction between human and animal.[29] He asserted that the simple act of throwing represented a fundamental difference in how humans and other animals perceived the world. His argument at the time was that with a lob or a toss, we humans learn to predict and control an element of the future. Aiming a stone or a spear, he argued, means that one is cognizant of and intends where the missile will land. Humans use their abilities to predict and control the future—something McDougall insisted that animals don't do. That's when I thought of Gretchen and her unique abilities that were as individual and honed as an Olympic javelin thrower's.

Floppy eared and with overstuffed feet, few things are as adorable as a German shepherd puppy. Gretchen, at eight weeks old, was no exception. I consider puppies much cuter and more interesting than kittens, so I admit my bias, but Gretchen was a phenomenal animal. Different from other dogs.

I was in graduate school at the time, and my schedule was flexible, if not lackadaisical. I could begin every day with an eight o'clock jog to the park with her. There, she learned to jump over obstacles, crawl through tunnels, and love the reward of catching her soft Frisbee. That was something I could do that she couldn't: throw an object. But she could do things I couldn't do, like track invisible footprints.

The more time I spent with Gretchen, the more the ostensible differences in cognition and personality blurred. My internal bias that there was a hierarchy of ability was cracking. Gretchen was a problem solver and a thinker. She could play—she was a dog—but she also reasoned in a way that seemed familiar to me. Other dogs I have known, such as fetch-obsessed border collies, seem to occupy their time with thoughts of "ball" or "stick." Gretchen, when she sat quietly, appeared to be puzzling something about the universe. I could see it in her eyes, as if she were examining the notion $E=mc^2$ . . . *That's mostly right, but there's something missing* . . . Deeper thought and being able to predict the future, I determined, were not something I could measure directly, but I could infer from observations of her behavior, especially from observing how she learned.

Gretchen was a quick and eager study. I taught her to jump up and over obstacles on command. To leap into water. To climb a ladder. We spent several years training and succeeded in becoming a search and rescue team for Larimer County Search and Rescue in Colorado.

One fun party trick was having her retrieve a beer for me from the refrigerator. It involved hearing the command, going into the kitchen, opening the refrigerator door, grabbing the beer, delivering the can, and then closing the refrigerator door. It was always a hit. Training a dog for a complicated task such as that requires an approach where the entire behavior is not taught at once. The whole thing is broken down into steps, each of which can be more easily learned one at a time and then linked like a chain.

To begin the training, I first played with Gretchen and a beer can, rolling it away and saying "beer." She already knew and enjoyed the game of fetch, so she linked the word with the can, and knew to bring it back to me when I called "beer." She also realized that too hard a mouth meant a puncture and bubbly spewing, so she quickly figured out on her own how to grip the can without putting a hole in it.

The next step was opening the refrigerator door. I tied a tug-of-war rope to the handle and dangled it before her. Commanding "open," she pulled on the rope to play. She tugged and the door opened. She looked surprised at first, as I immediately praised her for winning the game. After a few more trials, "open" clearly meant to her that she was to pull on the refrigerator door handle.

And this is where things got interesting. This is how I know that dogs, at least one German shepherd, can project into the future based on the past—not unlike McDougall's primeval human preparing to launch a spear.

I wasn't certain how I was going to link fetching a beer with opening the refrigerator door, and I assumed that it would take numerous trials to link the two completely different things in Gretchen's mind. To my astonishment, it required only one try. All I did was have Gretchen sit in front of the refrigerator. I showed her the beer can and then opened the door and placed it in the refrigerator. Then, I closed the door and commanded, "Beer."

Gretchen stood up, looked at me, and then at the refrigerator. She cocked her head and puzzled a few seconds. She pulled on the door handle. She opened the door, spied the beer inside—that she knew was there—grabbed it, and then brought it to me. She knew what was behind the door. She thought through the problem and solved it by properly putting together the linear steps. She could visualize; she could aim at the immediately invisible.

Scientific papers and discourse are essential, but I did not need anything more elaborate than one German shepherd to show me how dogs can reason, predict the future, and connect apparently disparate dots. But then, maybe all dogs can't reason and predict the future. Perhaps Gretchen was unique and many other dogs would not have been able to solve the puzzle. But that's the point, isn't it? Each dog has different abilities.

———

During my career I have worked mostly with coyotes—or at least with the imbroglios they cause—and I have built a mental scrapbook of animals and occurrences. Would I be losing my objectivity if I were to highlight my observations, acknowledging an attachment—a unique moment in time between two individuals—with a certain coyote or wolf?

I've captured, collared, and followed coyotes on research studies in Yellowstone National Park, the edge of the Great Basin near Lee Vining, California, and in the Sierra Nevada Mountains in the Lake Tahoe area. I spent seven years overseeing a research facility that housed hundreds of them and mentored many graduate students in studies on *Canis latrans*. Our lives—the little howling dogs' and mine—have long been intertwined not only scientifically but also personally.

I initially came to know individual coyotes much as most wild-life biologists do—through short encounters while capturing and fitting them with radio collars. The indispensable tool of wildlife research, especially for larger and secretive animals that wander widely, is the radio collar. Its signals allow biologists to observe animals even when the critters can't be seen. For my master's study, for example, I wanted to know if coyotes followed domestic sheep around, picking off stragglers, or if coyote territoriality kept a horde of marauders from developing. To track the domestic sheep, I put a collar on one in the flock. That was easy. Collaring the coyotes was a little trickier. Trapping coyotes is a challenging enterprise, and I had my own difficulties learning how to do it. I learned the most, of course, not when things went smoothly but rather when they went downhill rapidly.[30]

Personality-wise, most coyotes are submissive, and the reason they are often maligned as being pusillanimous lurkers is largely because they are. They may be predators, but as often as not they act more like wary and timid prey. Most eat voles and mice and rabbits and animals that have little ability to cause them harm. It is easy to become complacent about the predatory nature of coyotes when capturing and collaring them, because coyotes usually don't stand and fight when confronted; they abscond. Most coyotes, that is.

The typical capture involved cornering and pinning the re-strained animal. Their body pressed to the ground, they'd curl their tail submissively and not make eye contact. With these cues they indicated surrender, asked for mercy as if I was the dominant coyote in their pack. In those days I could speak at least that much coyote-ese. I'd act calmly and authoritatively as I pinned a trapped animal and then controlled it by wrapping my hand around its muzzle. Once held thus, its toothy weapons were neutralized. After that, it was a simple matter to wrap the self-sticking vet wrap around its mouth and use the same to hobble its legs together. Release the coyote from the trap, do a medical check and take measurements, put a radio collar on, and release. Like clockwork.

I found myself bonding with one coyote in a unique way, however.[31] It wasn't as if he were a submissive pet, but more like an equal. I don't know if he spit out the contents of the trap tranquilizer device, or if he just didn't care or feel its effects. He was most certainly different—an individual. He was not the cowering prey item most of his brethren appeared to be, but a large male coyote, a lord of the forest and field. This animal was not on the soft end of the prey to predator personality continuum; he was on the aggressive and surly side.

When I first pinned him, he fought more than most. Still, I was able to grab and wrap his muzzle fairly easily, having had more than a bit of experience in the procedure. I secured his legs, tying the front two together and then the back two. Immobilized, he rested, but only for a moment. When I stood up to reach past him for the radio collar, he lurched and brushed his muzzle across the ground. The movement swept the vet wrap off over his nose.

It was one of those moments when time slowed down.

I wailed, "Nooooooooooooooo," and reached down to grab the lurching coyote. The good news was that I was able to grab him before he was able to hop away. The bad news was that I was unable to grab the business end. I literally had a coyote by the tail. Worse yet, he was not interested in rolling over or running away in spite of my previous description of his species. He was hobbled but far from immobilized. He could hop and jump and lunge. Which he did. He snapped his fangs into my thigh.

I held his tail, but tried to keep him at an arm's distance so that he could not tear his teeth into my leg again. Or worse. His bite range was perilously close to my crotch. Our interaction turned into a dance. I held the base of his tail and suspended him above the ground just high enough to keep his lunges toward my groin ineffectual, but not so high that I was holding all his weight on his spine and perhaps hurting him. We went in circles until I was able to step forward with one of my boots to try to pin his muzzle down. It wasn't actually pinning, however, because he used the opportunity to latch his teeth into the thick rubber of my boot.

As he chewed on my inanimate sole, I was able to bring my other foot forward and pin his neck down. I contorted, reached gently between his ears, over his forehead, and wrapped my fingers around his muzzle. Finally, I had his mouth, which I sealed closed with a few rounds of electrical tape that I always had in my pocket.

The rest of the work went smoothly, and I put a collar on him and took a few measurements and notes. Then, I let him go, pushing him away as I released his muzzle. He lurched and leapt, then stopped to look back at me. He peed on a bush. At last he loped away. With my task safely finished, I dropped my pants and used gauze from the vet kit to treat my wounds. I kept direct pressure using electrical tape. I limped my way to the hospital a few hours later and tried to explain to the doctor why one living coyote was more important than the postexposure rabies vaccinations I was about to receive. The doctor didn't understand.

The interaction between that coyote and me was distinct, singular, and more significant than the length of its duration. All connections between human and animal are not necessarily in friendship, and they may be collaborative or more like predator and prey. Yet, unique and intense bonds are frequently created between us and them. That coyote was as individual as me, and my short relationship with him became a defining moment of my life. Was I less of a scientist for thinking this coyote was unique?

My internal bias about the unique superiority of humans was withering, but in its death it was birthing new thought. And in the development of a new worldview, I was not alone. To test my sanity and assumptions, I reached out to Lori Schmidt, the wolf curator at the International Wolf Center in Ely, Minnesota, who has known individual wolves as well as anyone has known their pet.[32] Her lifelong effort has resulted in a plethora of experience with an animal that most people know only from advertisements and nature shows. "I was in the right place at the right time," she says, her roots growing up on a farm resulted in a personal values system built on stewardship and an intense connection with nature. As a student, Schmidt did an internship with the Minnesota Department of Natural Resources researching moose and captive deer, which led to working in Ely. She met the famous wolf photographer Jim Brandenburg and researcher David Mech. Happening to live where the wolves were, she began working with them in 1986.

Her history on the farm gave Schmidt a practical view of the world, and from that perspective, a wolf is an efficient predator. Thus, she became interested in the functional aspects of behavior and how it leads to survival.

Schmidt works with wolves from all over, with different animals that could be considered subspecies, but she asserts that the subspecies concept is less relevant now: so much of what constitutes a wolf is wrapped up in the behavior of individuals as they navigate the environments where they live. Interviewing her helped me understand the transformation I was undergoing in assessing animal individuality and its importance. She explained that most behavioral variation is not between subspecies but rather in *how particular individuals in packs form their relationships with each other* and how the pack interacts with the local environment.

How did she come to her conclusions? The number of wolves she has closely worked with in her life may seem like a lot or surprisingly few. "Only about twenty-five," Schmidt says, "but I could name off each one." She goes on to point out that the Wolf Center is not a puppy mill; they don't breed at the center, but take in about two pups per year from other places, usually from another captive facility and not the wild. It's the responsibility of animal care that dampens the dream of Schmidt's otherwise envious job of working so closely with wolves. "There is no manual on how to interact with the pups that come in. Each one is different . . ." and she has to figure out how to interact with them.

Some wolves are social butterflies, flitting between humans and pack mates. Their bonds are broad but shallow. Other wolves grow up to be particularly reserved, very selective about whom they bonded with. A strong relationship between Schmidt and a wolf was real but rare, as she can name only three who significantly affected her life: Shadow, an Arctic wolf; Ballazar, a Great Plains wolf; and Aidan, the current dominant male at the center. Strong bonds between Schmidt and wolves happen only about 10 percent of the time. She tries to describe the relationships, but her words fall short. She says that a bond between a human and an animal isn't something easily described or quantified, and that the relationship between her and a wolf is more accurately described as a development of trust.

After providing a peek into her inner thoughts, Schmidt, ever professional, returns to her mission: "It is not about loving wolves, it is about the science and education." Schmidt loves and enjoys working with wolves, certainly, but she is not starry-eyed, sentimental, or self-righteous about it. Defining and measuring personality using an objective lens is like Odysseus navigating Scylla and Charybdis; researchers can't be so objective that we occlude our sight, and not so imaginative that we introduce bias.

"Here, the job is to give the facts," she says, referring to the whole of biology and the International Wolf Center's mission. "There are issues of carrying capacity, disease, and how to die versus not being allowed to reproduce. We can only educate people about wolves in the larger context." She proselytizes the science, but explicitly avoids dictating morality or how to think. "People have to apply their values onto the knowledge that we provide." Nature has rules—some win and some lose—and nature has limits: even Yellowstone has a carrying capacity of wolves that is regulated through disease, misfortune, and bloody battle. Schmidt's thoughts knock me back on my heels. Yes, wolves are magnificent and beautiful, but there is more to it than that. There is much to discover in Schmidt's hints about individual variation, but she stops short of giving me all the answers. Awarded for her teaching, Schmidt notes that the best teachers "show you where to look and not what to see."

Motivated to learn more about others' thoughts on wolves, I read *Wild Wolves We Have Known*, edited by Richard Thiel, Allison Thiel, and Marianne Strozewski, and I found strength in numbers.[33] The book is an anthology of reminiscences by wolf biologists from all around the world. The recollections are poignant—reflecting the personalities of the people doing the research as much as the nature of individual wolves. They are stories of wonder and adventure, but they also highlight that I am not the only scientist who feels this way. Other scientists too have cherished the individual and formed particular bonds with a specific wolf.

The extraordinary wolf researcher, Dave Mech named the bold young wolf of Ellesmere Island Brutus, it being immediately apparent that the animal sniffing the famous biologist's glove was no ordinary wolf.[34] Adrian Wydeven's venerable Wolf 475 roamed with Wisconsin's Shanagolden pack. Rick McIntyre described the famous Yellowstone National Park 06 Female's plight. She was first followed as a lone wolf, then a pack leader and mother. She became renowned as a great hunter of elk, killing the large ungulates by herself. She met her end tragically when she was legally shot and killed on December 6, 2012, after transgressing park boundaries, moving from protected animal to trophy species by crossing an invisible line. Her death provoked palpable international outrage, because so many people knew her for who she was: an individual with her own story.

My favorite story was perhaps Maggie Dwire's "A Tail of a Wolf." In it, the male Mexican wolf 732 provided the most vivid of anecdotes, being observed closely in both captivity and the wild. First, he was allowed to have a name, Bob. Bob was an individual with a story, which included having a hard life—certainly, being an endangered species sets one back—and being born with a stubby tail that led to his sobriquet. Whelped at the Sevilleta Wolf Management Facility in Socorro, New Mexico, Bob was released into the wild with his family when he was a youngster. Things went downhill rapidly after that. Bob's father was killed by a truck on the highway. His mother injured her foot and needed to be recaptured. His brother ran off with a wild female. Bob, who would have been as aptly named Job, persevered and set up camp out of the wolf recovery area—at a dump. This led to his assignation in the ignoble category of "not likely to assist in the recovery effort." He was recaptured and brought back to Sevilleta within ten weeks of tasting freedom.

Back at Sevilleta, Bob was introduced to his future mate, Female 797. He rushed into her pen and ran toward her pups. She promptly decked him. Then again. And again. Bob was eventually able to approach her on his belly, rolling over on his back before her. They were strikingly different in personality: where she was domineering and aggressive, he was submissive, diffident. When she was captured for handling and release, she would fight with the biologists. Bob, as if he were one of her pups, immediately acquiesced. It primed me for what I came to understand later: that some animals are aggressive and bold, and others are more timid and meek—but that neither strategy is optimal in all instances.

Released into the wild for a second chance, Bob and his bold mate began killing livestock. That behavior drastically shortened his predicted life span through the institution of what is known as a removal order. Wearing a radio collar, he was easy to find, and they flew in a plane after him. They shot him from the air and left him for dead. Soon after, however, biologists realized that his radio collar kept moving. Bob was alive. They brought in the plane the second time. This time they confirmed his death. To everyone's surprise, his radio collar continued to wander the landscape with him, as relentless as the undead. They flew again. They shot Bob. Biologists hiked in a day later and found proof of his demise: a detached radio collar, bloodied and bullet torn.

Biologists continued to monitor his mate, however, who was raising their young pups. They provided her supplemental food and installed trail cameras nearby to observe her and her pups. She looked odd in one set of pictures. More than odd for a mother wolf. The photographs were of a male wolf, uncollared and stub-tailed. Bob was alive. Bob was not bold, but he was persistent—another personality type that I would eventually learn to acknowledge and study. Bob was unique among all others of his kind, even as rare as they were.

The final prod I received from *Wild Wolves* was a first hint at the danger of preconceived notions, of continuing to force individuals into a behavioral box. Juan Carlos Blanco and Yolanda Cortés tell the tale of European wolves, one in particular, Ernesto, who bore little resemblance to a big, bad wolf. He worked around the edges of humanity, consuming carcasses of livestock rather than killing them. He lived in a treeless agricultural landscape. The idea of a species as magnificent as the wolf comporting in the manor of a lowly scavenger was too much for some, however. As quoted by Blanco and Cortés, Gordon Haber (the passionate Alaska wolf biologist tragically lost in a plane crash in 2009) most definitely had an opinion about the Spanish wolves, asking, "Should . . . garbage-eating, largely solitary, sunflower-field canids really be regarded as wolves? Or are they the product of a lengthy, subtle process of 'unwolving'?"[35] To Haber, if a wolf didn't conform to his personal archetype, it wasn't a wolf. Such bias is dangerous too: to accept that wolves have different personalities means that both the lay public and scientists have to be fully open to the idea of variety—whatever the result. Some wolves are bold and macho, brutal killers of dogs. Some wolves are pusillanimous, feckless dump divers. Loving an idea of what wolves represent is not the same as understanding what a wolf is. One must also accept their individuality.

———

Learning that I wasn't the only wildlife researcher who recognized the uniqueness of individual wolves helped me as I endeavored to shed the dogma inculcated within me. A hurdle remained, however—a covert bias. Not prejudice, as I've since awakened from my Morganistic opioids, but perceptive bias: the simple fact that the human sensory map of the world is so different from animals'. Again, it wasn't the scientific literature where I discovered my limitations but in my relationship with my dog.

Gretchen and I started one morning with first steps through morning dew. My footprints looked like photographic negatives, green prints defined in hazy gray dew. I began training Gretchen to follow her nose, to track on command. I would tell her to stay and then I'd walk away and place small treats within my footprints. Commanding "search," I first set her along the short path, with a reward of chasing a flying disk at the end. She put her nose down, sniffing the ground. She smelled my print, found the treat. Moving forward, she swung her nose to the next print. "Good girl," I encouraged her. Nose to print, nose to print, she found another treat randomly. When she understood the game, I lengthened the trails and held off on the treats, rewarding with just the toy. Gretchen eventually learned to sniff the wind, smelling people hundreds of yards away. There it was, right in front of me: an obvious indicator that a wall of perceptive differences stood between us.

I imagined having the sensory capability of a dog. Millions of scent receptors that painted a picture of the landscape in odors. Then I read of the work of Kathryn Payne, and how elephants communicate across vast distances using infrasound, frequencies far below humans' ability to hear. Scientists didn't even discover such a fundamental aspect of elephant behavior until the 1980s.[36] Beyond my observations, research was growing that showed how pathetic human senses are when compared to the capabilities of animals. We humans may think they are dumb or can't do the things we do, but science really doesn't even know what the skill sets of most animals actually are. To borrow again from the physicists, more dark matter is turning behavioral orbits of other species; people can't experience animals' perceptive frameworks, but to understand their potential motivations we have to acknowledge that their realities are different from ours.

Sight is the primary means by which we experience the world around us. The sensory world of a dog is starkly different.[37] As you walk your dog, you may intermittently pause with your phone to check e-mail or Facebook. Your dog, however, will lope from place to place, checking "Peemail" and "Nosebook."[38] What is a billboard of olfactory information to a dog and many other species is absolutely invisible to us. In a dog's sensory world, a patch of yellow snow may read like a placard of information: species, gender, age and identity of the interloper, including when they last visited. Humans had to learn to write in order to share the information that dogs naturally broadcast all over the neighborhood. They get it all from a sniff. Not only do they have twenty times as many primary scent receptors as humans and some crazy differences in sensory ability, but they also have a functional vomeronasal organ, like a second nose, which humans don't have the benefit of either. Opposable thumbs; how ordinary.

So, can people smell like a dog, see like a snake, or feel vibration like a spider? No, ours is our own sensory world. We have to be cautious about projecting onto other species interpretations of behavior based on our sensory inputs. Our perception of color is likely better than a dog's but pales relative to an eagle's. If researchers design a test for detecting shades, a dog will fail where humans will do well and eagles will excel, but if they design a test for detecting smells, Fido will rule and humans and raptors will fail. Humans are completely blind to the olfactory world that dogs and reptiles inhabit.

I read how Laura McShane and her coauthors listened to the unintelligible screams, whines, whistles, squeaks, squeals, and whimpers of sea otters.[39] Overcoming limitations of the human ear by creating sonograms, and using open minds, the scientists could identify individual otters by their voices. If we humans can tell otters apart with our poor instruments, most certainly they can tell one from another with their specifically tuned ears. For the longest time we didn't know to listen for elephants communicating using sounds below the range of human hearing.[40] The tactile abilities of even the smallest creatures are wondrous, be it water striders in a pond or the way flies so adeptly (if not always perfectly) know a swat is coming long before its arrival. What other signs and signals are we unable to observe? What other abilities do we miss?

Take the mirror test, for example. It's one that researchers use to prove whether or not other animals have self-consciousness. The mirror test doesn't work for many species, but if we put a dab of paint on an elephant's forehead and let it study itself in the mirror, some elephants will reach for their forehead based on their reflection in the mirror. They know it is their reflection. It's difficult to do this with a dog; this may be an effect of an intense human bias toward vision that dogs may not have. A dog, for instance, may not know itself by how it looks but rather by how it smells. Give a person an olfactory mirror test with our own odors, and we'll fail. If researchers find a way to give a dog an olfactory mirror test, I would not be surprised if they know exactly who they are as individuals. The more I discover about animal perception, the more I learn how much I don't know.

What I've decided as a scientist is not to discount a concept or hypothesis just because scientists don't have complete intellectual mastery over it. It has put me into the right frame of mind to try different lenses, to break away from the restrictive dogma, to "Doolittle" a little. Indeed, in his response to the overinstitutionalism of Morgan, the Cambridge professor Patrick Bateson noted as early as the late 1980s that "slavish obedience to such a maxim . . . tends to sterilize imagination. When an animal is thought of as a piece of clockwork machinery, then some of its most interesting attributes are almost certainly overlooked."[41]

Given the limitations of earlier scientific zeitgeist and the reluctance to accept similarities between humans and other animals, it is unfortunate but not surprising that the study of personality in animals has not expanded into a discipline of its own. Scientists have been defensive and shy in the shadow of Morgan, and we continue to use vapid phrases such as *behavioral syndromes*, instead of *personality*. We've deadened the language and lost some ability to communicate findings. If we don't resurrect Darwin's thoughts and prioritize individual emotion and personality in the context of natural selection again, we'll lose another opportunity to better understand the species with which humans share this planet. Happily, scientists are now boldly moving forward in this new, fertile field.

The Mystery of Personality

The radiant setting sun lights the sky on fire over a gorgeous panorama of beach, refracting through the beads of condensation on my beer glass. With the comfort of a twilight beverage, I'm watching the waves and resting on the deck at Amplified Ale Works in San Diego. My loved ones are far away, shoveling distant Utah snows, but missing them keeps me from feeling smug in the luxury of Southern Californian climate. I'm living in the moment, enjoying the drink and the scene, but I think that something is different about me, pampered but unsatisfied. I can't shake the feeling that traveling for business, even to exotic locations, is still drudgery.

Is it that I am social and want to be near people? But I am sitting alone. I'm shy, not even leaning to strike up a conversation with any of those in the pub around me. Am I asocial and solo? But I'm thinking of who I miss. Am I adventurous and bold, because at a moment's notice I filled Pingüino's bowl and flew half way across the country to brief a gaggle of policymakers about the intersection of biology and politics? They are colleagues and business acquaintances, but not my friends; I don't want to relax with them, but I don't want to fight with them either, so I have opted for a beer, fries, and a solitary sunset.

I am forced from my indulgent introspection when a woman at the table behind me says, "Look at my cat! Isn't he the coolest ever?" Her first sentence a demand, the second not a question but a conclusion. She waves her cell phone about the table, displaying a picture of a cat lounging on her rug.

Overcoming my shyness, I interject, "No, I don't think so." Pingüino's picture is the background on my phone. The complacent bastard is resting peacefully, neck deep into the buffalo throw that covers the back of my couch. His lids droop heavily, like the smoky eyes of a seductive courtesan, and his left paw is outstretched, the claws kneading the depths of fur. The guy has no self-doubt and no regrets. I flash the picture above the woman and display him to her table.

"Boom," I say, confidently. "Yours doesn't have this personality. The dude has *attitude*." Those at the table laugh, and the woman grins. I know that I am victorious—and, yes, smug. But aren't we all when it comes to our animal companions?

The moment culminates a notion. I have a cat whom I have somehow bonded with, and it isn't because of his lopsided whiskers or his alarming purring. It isn't because I am crazy either, imagining connections that aren't there. Pingüino is a cat, and to a great extent he rolls solo, but as further evidence of our link, I think of a previous morning. I had stretched in bed and Pingüino had jumped to my side, snuggling with me and purring. He brought his nose to mine and meowed as softly as he could (that is to say, loudly). In my foggy dawn mind, he was showing me all the signs: clearly communicating that he loved me. He continued, meowing and purring and hopping around. It was lovely, but as my thoughts cleared, I realized that my initial dreamy-eyed story of him expressing affection was not his sole motivation. I arose and walked into the hall. He followed me, then dashed ahead.

I filled his empty food bowl. While brewing the morning coffee, I thought, Pingüino loves food, not me. I considered the danger of overinterpreting intent in animals as my cautious inner scientist told my emotions to back off. Then the warm and bitter sips of French roast slapped me upside the head. He had many options that morning of how he could have communicated. He could have curled up in another part of the house, avoiding me, but he didn't. Running to the food did not preclude anything else about the bond between him and me. I was a provider, yes, but his actions showed that he *trusted* me.

I am not crazy for noting that Pingüino and I have a relationship that is distinct from the bond I've had with any other, be it human, dog, or cat. Indeed, every animal is an individual, and not just charismatic megafauna, such as elephants, wolves, or whales; every dog, cat, horse, crab, water strider, salamander, and spider is distinct. Within the essence of our distinctiveness, fortunately, we have the additional ability to single each other out as friends or foes. We have chemistry; we learn, trust, and form the bonds that arise from complementary strengths of entirely unique personalities—human or not.

The sun has set over both Salt Lake and San Diego, and my beer is finished, but Pingüino and I remain bonded. Our relationship is especially ironic because I am not a cat person, but I've somehow ended up playing that role. I can forgive myself, because Pingüino is different. Together, we have created a team. He trusts me. I trust him. I know this to be true, but still struggle with the task of describing us, using words that fall far short in their precision: Exactly who are he and I?

What is personality? A Google definition says it's "the characteristics that make up a person's distinctive character." That doesn't seem helpful. How would a scientist measure that? Defining personality is challenging because it is not easily quantifiable nor is it a physical thing that you can poke with a scalpel. Personality is an elusive alchemy of the identifiable and ineffable. It is stable, but also malleable. It has to be consistent to be demonstrable, but paradoxically, it can't be static, robotic programming. We accept it intuitively—differences between other individuals in the same situation—but we can't measure it succinctly, like height or weight. Defining personality is like Justice Stewart's "I know it when I see it" definition of pornography.

Indeed, quantifying personality has been problematic since scientists have shown interest in studying it. In 1996, for instance, Stephen Suomi, Melinda Novak, and Arnold Well published a paper on personality in rhesus monkeys, but the word *personality* is buried in the document, which was enigmatically titled, "Aging in Rhesus Monkeys: Different Windows on Behavioral Continuity and Change."[1] The analyses and results are not readily accessible to the general public, or even to many biologists, unless they are familiar with mixed design analysis of variance and orthongonal-polynomial contrasts. Critical mass can't be achieved and the discipline can't build momentum when the studies are subject to jargon and statistical speak, so I will focus on the interpretation of the results and not the analysis.

The researchers began their study in the year that the Viking Lander touched down on Mars, the year when a tiny company called Apple Computers was started and the United States injected a quaint currency, the two dollar bill, into circulation. In 1976 the Animal Welfare Act was receiving its second tweak to protect animals from being transported across state lines for fighting ventures, and eight monkeys at the University of Massachusetts Primate Laboratory were given a little extra attention by Suomi, Novak, and Well. The animals weren't being poked and prodded, but in a landmark effort, were being systematically ranked not by physiology but by behavior. Who was a solo loner or aggressive or collegial, for example. The work, a nascent form of personality research, followed the individuals from six years old until they were twenty in 1990.

At first glance, the data indicated each animal changed through time, which leads to more than a little confusion and skepticism when trying to pin down what an animal personality is. The stimulus-response behaviorists would have been right if all animals identically altered their behaviors when conditions changed. The definition of personality has to anchor to the uniqueness of an individual, with elements that remain consistent through time. Some scientists even declare that the only way to prove that personality exists requires finding a genetic component that creates it. We will examine that assertion more fully later, but for now we can determine if we come to the same conclusions the University of Massachusetts researchers did.

The researchers combed the data for trends, looking for them as they would if researching differences between individual humans. All three of the males studied were passive in their interactions with others; they were nonsocial most of the time. The females were much more outgoing: two of them had contact with other animals as their prime activity, and every female was more social than every male. Females were more likely to interact with their environment, fiddling with objects using their hands and mouths. The males were more solitary and their behaviors frequently involved hierarchical displays—determining who's the dominant one in the room. If I spent my training trying to resist anthropomorphizing, well, here I can't resist the temptation to zoomorphize: the research results describe my office staff meetings.

The most intriguing aspect of the study, however, was not the differences between the sexes. What the researchers did that was so novel was to measure an individual's response not just as a snapshot in time. They dipped into the pool of personality potential by tracking the animals through the years and recognizing the consistency and uniqueness of individuals. Age acted on rhesus monkeys much as it does on humans. The daring discovery admitted by Suomi and colleagues was that the monkeys' behaviors were affected, but not wholly altered, by time. An aggressive jerk as a youngster became a bit mellower, but he was still an aggressive jerk in late adulthood. Personality differs between animals and stays consistent, but is shaped by time. The researchers concluded that "there was remarkable consistency within individual behavioral profiles across the entire study such that each monkey retained its distinctive behavioral features (personality) throughout its adult years."[2] Acknowledging that consistency was science's first step toward an accepted study of animal personality.

The destruction left in Hurricane Katrina's wake, dystopian in degree and scale, changed the landscape and left a feeling of insecurity for both human and animal. At the Marine Life Oceanarium in Gulfport, Mississippi, Katrina left only a skeletal hulk, girders stripped naked of their canopies. The Oceanarium's above-ground infrastructure was a wasteland. Katrina's rage was not limited to the swirling winds, as waters also scoured the ground and flayed open steel and concrete pools. Nothing was impervious to the destruction. Nature, weather, is a fickle and heartless thing. Many ancient civilizations developed powerful and capricious gods to explain such natural anger, arbitrarily rewarding with plenty on one day and then punishing with destruction on another. The planet and universe cast so much adversity at life. But if there is a silver lining and lesson in the horror, it is that life is resilient. Life adapts.

Before the storm, staff at the Oceanarium had evacuated many of the facility's animals, but they could not move them all. About half of the dolphins were moved to a secure location, but eight were left in a pool on site with the assumption that their home would be secure. When the staff returned to the mangled mess, the eight dolphins were gone. During the Katrina catastrophe, the Oceanarium's pools were overrun and the pod of beloved bottlenose dolphins was swept away through twisted wreckage and floodwaters. The dolphins survived and surfaced in the Gulf, miraculously, without suffering massive injuries.

It is said that the dolphins flipped with joy when they were found, disoriented and hungry, by their trainers. Raised in captivity, they did not have the skills to fend for themselves in the waters of the Gulf coast. The dolphins did what they knew how to do, and they waited for the people with whom they had created bonds.

To rescue the dolphins, the staff first fortified the aquatic mammals with vitamin-stuffed fish treats to get their strength back. Then they were asked to swim prone onto a tarp, which was used to lift and transport them: first to a hotel swimming pool, then to temporary pools provided by the US Navy. Ultimately all the animals were reunited at the Atlantis Resort in the Bahamas.

Scientists had the unique opportunity to examine these fifteen bottlenose dolphins and their response to the tragedy wrought by Katrina. All the original dolphins (twelve females and four males; half born in the wild, half in captivity) had been part of a previous research study in which their personalities were assessed by graduate students and Marine Life Oceanarium trainers. The trainers had spent the better part of a year, a couple of weeks at a time, assessing the dolphins for certain traits based on the NEO-PI, a human-calibrated five-factor personality assessment: openness to experience, conscientiousness, extroversion, agreeableness, and neuroticism. Trainers judged the dolphins independently and were instructed not to share notes about their impressions of their subjects.

In the prestorm assessment, human observers came to the same, statistically significant conclusions about a dolphin's five-factor description. When raters did disagree on a dolphin's score on a seven-point scale of having the trait versus not, the average difference in ratings was only one point—a minor difference in degree of a trait. All the voters, though, agreed that the dolphins possessed these traits. It was quantitatively clear that different dolphins were different, but in ways that could be described using a personality scale developed for humans. Dolphin H (identified by letter, genuflecting to Morgan Canon's demand for the appearance of objectivity, although I am inclined to believe that the animal had an actual name) was not a dolphin I'd be likely to hang out with. A seventeen-year-old female, she ranked moderate to low on openness, conscientiousness, extroversion, and agreeableness, but was the second highest for neuroticism. I think I'd get along better with G, the nine-year-old female who was lower on openness, highly conscientious, not at all extroverted, very agreeable, and by far the lowest in terms of neuroticism. I am by definition anthropomorphizing the hell out of these animals by saying I think that G and I have much in common, but I didn't categorize the animals, scientists did.

Then, Katrina came and destroyed the dolphins' world. The destruction was terrible, but it presented researchers with a unique opportunity to examine the strength of each animal's personality. Did the individuals keep their distinguishing patterns of behavior after a traumatic event and in new and completely different surroundings? Post-Katrina, the dolphins had been moved multiple times, housed in small pools, separated and reunified, and then moved to a new environment in the Bahamas.

The series of very unfortunate events created the conditions of a quasi-experiment, and researchers at the University of Southern Mississippi wisely spied the opportunity and took advantage of it. Specifically, Lauren Highfill and Stan Kuczaj II gave the human evaluators at the dolphins' abode in the Bahamas the same five-factor-based definitions with which to evaluate each dolphin. Once again, the judges were consistent in how they rated individuals, with only an average one-point difference in degree of a trait. Were the dolphins' personalities consistent with their prestorm selves?

The answer is mostly yes, but not always. Eleven of the fifteen dolphins had pre- and post-Katrina personality scores that were highly correlated. Some, however, did not fare so well. Dolphin G ranked the highest in conscientiousness and agreeableness and low-est in neuroticism before the storm, but differed dramatically after. She flipped completely, becoming the least conscientious and agree-able, with a high ranking for neuroticism. She had been affected by the trauma.

There were two conclusions to be made from the observations of the dolphins. The first was that personality survives even after a horrendous trauma. It is a real phenomenon that defines individu-als through time. Individuals are unique, and their behaviors retain similar patterns and characteristics through time. Something anchors dolphins, humans, and all animals in our personalities, something innate and genetic in expression. But another, less comforting con-clusion can be made too. Even with the best schematics and basis of behavior, our emotional wiring can short-circuit. We are not prepro-grammed robots with unlimited resilience. People and dolphins are susceptible to tragedy. Dolphin G, in changing so much before and after Katrina, likely experienced a phenomenon that scientists have only recently given its due in humans: post-traumatic stress disorder.

If some aspects of an animal's personality change, how do we mea-sure with any certain detail the plastic dynamic trend that is person-ality? It's one thing to say that a coyote is scrappy and aggressive, but another to determine what scrappy and aggressive actually mean on an individual or relative scale. We have to be careful with ter-minology and meaning. "Scrappy" or "aggressive" are commonly measured as "boldness," meaning a propensity to take risks. But the context is important too. Sometimes boldness more precisely means to take risks in novel situations, but other times it is interpreted as response to known risks. Boldness can be tested by recording re-sponses to a novel object, for instance, or to direct predation risk. Alecia Carter, at the Fenner School of Environment and Society at the Australian National University in Canberra, wrote about poten-tial pitfalls of loose terminology in the nascent discipline of animal personality, especially when using singular terms such as boldness to describe a wide variety of behaviors and contexts.[3] At its worse, we can erroneously portray—or fail to detect—behavioral types and variations in species because of misapplied language. We scientists have to be aware of the ramifications that may result due to the imprecision in our labels.

The scientists who were beginning to acknowledge the existence of personality in mammals were also beginning to face the challenges that psychologists had long been struggling with in their attempts to quantify human personality, and the approaches made by psychologists merit their own book or course of study.[4] Although they have been unfettered by Morgan's Canon, psychologists still have not been able to agree on universal metrics. They have also tended to focus on psychopathy and destructive behaviors rather than individual variation per se. Psychologists have subjects whom they can talk to, reason with, and even share the same physiology with, but they still can't figure out exactly what is going on in someone else's mind. It's obvious that people differ, but how are those normal differences quantified? The extremes are easy: a mass murderer is a psychopath, a humanitarian a saint, a selfless soldier a hero. The day-to-day differences between individuals are more difficult to measure, yet scientists and laypeople alike are compelled to try. Expanding science into popular culture, online and magazine quizzes help people identify where they fit in. What Disney character are you? Which superhero? Which Shakespeare character? (I could not resist; one quiz concluded that I'm Rosalind from *As You Like It*).

The irony of how science measures and demonstrates individual personality is that we do it by grouping individuals into categories. To make sense of the world requires being at least somewhat reductionist about it. There are a variety of commonly used instruments for assessing personality in people. They are worthy of discussion here, because they provide a framework on which to map animal personality, even if a wolf can't answer survey questions.

First, and probably the most well known, is the Myers-Briggs Type Indicator. It relies on subjects to respond to a series of questions, and the answers are used to construct a matrix of scored attributes. Jung first boiled people down to basic categories of introverts and extraverts[5] from which Isabel Briggs Myers and her mother, Katharine Briggs, expanded to include extraversion versus introversion, sensing versus intuition, thinking versus feeling, and judging versus perceiving. Derived labels identify sixteen possible combinations of these basic types.[6] A person's essence is reduced to a four-lettered category of ENFJ (extraversion, intuition, feeling, judging). More specifically, the extraversion-introversion continuum measures whether someone turns outward toward external action or inward toward thought. The sensing-intuition continuum attempts to measure whether someone is more likely to use her senses to interpret new information or to evaluate it internally, comparing observations with intuition. The thinking-feeling continuum evaluates the *Star Trek* Vulcan within us, who makes decisions based on rational thought, versus someone who employs empathy. Finally, the judging-perceiving continuum examines how a person relates to the outside world by preferring to come to conclusions based on gathered information versus continuing to gather more information.

Another model of personality, the NEO PI, uses a different set of categories in what is known as a five-factor model, and was the system adapted to study the dolphins of Katrina. The first factor is openness to experience: ranking high when an animal is creative and imaginative and addresses problems in a novel way; ranking low when it engages in routine behaviors without a complex behavioral repertoire. The second factor, conscientiousness, ranges from careful and cautious to being inconsistent or unpredictable. Third, extroversion, is ranked from assertive and self-assured to relatively unresponsive to stimuli. Fourth, agreeableness means being friendly and gentle, not hostile and kind to others at the high end and selfish and self-centered at the low end. The fifth factor, neuroticism, is apparent when an animal is jealous or resentful of others but is low when an individual is tolerant and easy going.

The Minnesota Multiphasic Personality Inventory was first published and used in the 1940s, and then revised in 1989, to establish the MMPI-2. It is the most widely used psychometric test for evaluating adult psychopathology.[7] The tool strives to negate personal attempts to outsmart it and to appear in a more positive light by using nine "lying" scales that measure lying, defensiveness, faking good, and faking bad, as well as clinical scales that evaluate potential mental health problems such as depression, anxiety, post-traumatic stress disorder, psychopathy, and more general personality traits, such as anger, hypochondriasis, and addiction potential. Widely used clinically, the test, with 567 true or false items, is more appropriate for trained psychologists and less directly adaptable to identifying animal personality.

The Eysenck Personality Questionnaire is similar to the others in that it classifies scales for psychoticism (P), extraversion (E), neuroticism (N), and a social desirability or lie scale (L). Psychoticism is associated with aggressiveness. Extraversion is how it is normally thought of: characterized by being outgoing, talkative. Neuroticism is essentially emotionality and the L is the attempt to evaluate a respondent's desire to outsmart the test.

The strength of the personality tests is in their attempt to be objective, even though they fall short of being completely unbiased. They allow us to begin to parse out demonstrable elements of personalities. One weakness, however, is that they require self-reporting, and even with lie factors, people are not objective evaluators of themselves. Some psychologists attempted to peer more directly into the underlying personality, the subconscious, by analyzing responses to meaningless inkblots, such as in the Rorschach test, but it relies on an individual's interpretation, response, and communication. Ultimately the psychological tests are useful because they provide a framework, and in the chapters that follow we will see how scientists are using the five-factor model (an adapted NEO-PI) and the Myers-Briggs categories to define individuals, especially to fine-tune the precision of notions about personality.

Those studying animal behavior have also relied on additional categories to help them identify trends in behavioral variation. Samuel Gosling, at the University of Texas, Austin, and his coauthors wrote one of the initial breakout papers in 2003 about personality, and his lab continues to lead in the field. Using the framework of a five-factor model, but finding no translation of conscientiousness in animal behavior, he identified four factors, energy (analogous to extroversion), affection (agreeableness), emotional reactivity (neuroticism), and intelligence (openness/intellect), and showed how they could be repeatedly and reliably assessed in different dogs by different people.[8]

More recent literature on animal behavior has divided animals into other continua, elements related to those identified above, that can be repeatedly measured with observation and not questionnaires. The categories and descriptions transcend species, families, and phyla. The bold-shy continuum is usually expressed in the context of external dangers. Some coyotes are very wary, afraid of anything new and potentially dangerous, while others are more inquisitive than wary. The continuum from aggressiveness to passivity is essentially the difference between a fighter and a lover: some bluebirds attack others relentlessly, for example, and others are more tolerant of intrusions. Solitary or social is evident in species of spiders where some individuals live in groups benefiting from communal webs, whereas others strike out on their own for their own reasons. There are the adventurers versus the homebodies: some larval salamanders explore the wider world whereas others stay hidden and close to home. We will investigate them all in the coming pages

Being individuals, we humans each have narratives and use our own stories to map our place in the world. I have recently determined that I am an ENTJ.[9] To be more precise, I barely fall into the extravert category, overwhelmingly prefer intuition over sensing, tend to be more thinking than feeling, and favor judging over perceiving. As such, I am in great company, sharing the personality type with notables such as Franklin D. Roosevelt, Richard M. Nixon, Jim Carrey, Rahm Emanuel, Harrison Ford, Newt Gingrich, Whoopi Goldberg, Benny Goodman, Al Gore, Steve Jobs, Dave Letterman, Steve Martin, General Norman Schwarzkopf, and Patrick Stewart. I am relieved to report that Hitler was an INFJ.[10]

That is the limitation, the double-edged sword of using the tests. Hitler may have been an INFJ, but that does not mean that all INFJs—and no others—have the capacity to be genocidal maniacs. An ironic characteristic of all personality tests is that they describe individuals by partitioning them into categories and may not even describe the most important aspect of the individual. Personality types are imperfect models; that is, they are stories we use to relate to and understand others. It is like studying snowflakes, which can also be put into thirty-five or so categories, but any one category does not completely define the individual.[11]

Do we need the perfect experiment and definition? No, we don't need to know everything about every individual to understand individuality, but the tests and categories do help us organize and understand the world. An ENTJ is not a complete truth about who I am, but it does provide a framework with which to begin to understand me. Personality categories are used not as an end in themselves but as tools in a larger narrative.

I don't have the presence of Patrick Stewart and am not as funny as Steve Martin or as politically paranoid as Richard Nixon. As a scientist, I seek out intellectual stimulation, not because I am particularly smart but because learning about animals and their behaviors is enjoyable. Yes, ironically, and perhaps contrary to popular belief, scientists seek out rationality for irrational reasons. Scientists can have fun. Scientists can even have personality, be cool.

Scientists seek out intellectual pursuits because we have a passion for them; sometimes we become obsessed by our research. Because we feel at our best when we communicate our discoveries, we agree to meet on common ground that we call objectivity. Although we have a passion for the animals and the research, at some point, studies and knowledge have to be forced through the filter of objectivity. Sometimes objectivity is quantitative, measurable, and relatively easy: such as weight or height or the number of times an animal did a certain thing.

For the bigger questions, however, dry objectivity without analysis and interpretation is not enough. Science has to rely on other tools, such as stories, too. Scientists try to be as objective as possible—but we use stories nonetheless. One can't *see* evolution, but we infer its storyline from the bits and pieces we do see: similarity in animals, breeding experiments, DNA. Even the most quantitative of quantitative physicists use stories. Physicist Erwin Schrödinger, in his famous thought experiment explaining an inference from quantum theory, told the story of a cat that was simultaneously both dead and alive. So stories in science are not necessarily bad things.

A story led to my own addiction to the study of animal behavior. When I was a sophomore in college, my professor was explaining how a complicated and improbable mating ritual could evolve in a species of fly. Why would, for instance, *Empis sartor* males create a great ball of silk to seduce females? The task was a large one, and surely didn't evolve all at once, with one clever male suddenly deciding to create a great cocoon as a present for a lady fly.

The story that captivated me linked together related fly species' sequential approaches to courtship. In a basic mating ritual, *E. trigramma* males have a delicate choice to balance; females view the males as prey as much as mates.[12] So, an *E. trigramma* male, when finding a female, will follow her and wait until she is eating something else before attempting to copulate. Her attention on the meal increases his odds of surviving his attempt to pass on his genes. Males of the species *E. poplitea* improved the system a bit. Rather than passively waiting for the female to find prey, an *E. poplitea* male will find a morsel, such as another fly, and present it to the female. Distracted (and nourished) by the food, she doesn't kill him and lets him mate with her—if he is fast enough. If the prey is small or consumed quickly, the males don't transfer as much sperm and are still likely to be eaten. To slow the female's feast, another closely related species, *Hilara quadrivittata*, increases his odds further by wrapping the meal in a cocoon before he presents it to the female. She has to spend time unwrapping before eating, which further increases the male's probability of both sexual success and survival. The male of *H. thoracica* makes a big and elaborate cocoon to keep her occupied even longer, but takes time only to put a small treat in the center. You may see where this is going: *H. maura* generally include prey in their cocoon gifts, but some deadbeats don't even bother to capture prey; they only distract the duped female into digging into a gift with useless contents, such as a flower petal, while the male mates and flies. Perhaps this could be an example of lazy versus industrious, but the story progresses, until ultimately, an *H. sartor* male only ceremonially presents a silken cocoon to the female who accepts the gift like a wedding cake.

Science can't rewind the passage of time to watch each step in the evolution of a behavior, but we can, argued such venerable founders of the study of animal behavior as Konrad Lorenz, use this comparative method to look for the connections among species and to infer the whole logical story.[13] Different species, living in their own particular ecological niches, create their own storylines of how best to survive.

———

The desert tortoise in front of me is named Rose. She is like a green flower, a half orb of deliberative movement. Scaled, stubby legs extend from her body like rough petals. It is not the half dome of her carapace, however, nor the comely round pupils above her Mona Lisa smile that define her as a work of art. Where we humans may be avariciously envious of her is that we cannot achieve her reptile Zen and become the slow-moving wisdom that is a desert tortoise. Rose will easily live fifty years, so she has time to think about stretching for each two-inch step, and she doesn't worry, being an armored, unavailable prey. She shows the nonchalance of her age and lack of concern sometimes when she absentmindedly leaves a blade of grass drooping from her chin like a stale cigarette on the lip of a gone-in-the-teeth grandma.

"I saw a random segment on the Internet," Denise Cheung smiles diffidently.[14] "That's how we ended up with Rose."

A "threatened" species under the protection of the Endangered Species Act, desert tortoises are not pet store chattel, like the lizards and snakes or fish that fill strip mall aquariums. Rather, they are adopted only rarely, such as when, for various reasons, they cannot be returned to the wild. Rose, for example, has an injury to her shell, and one of her rhomboidal scutes has been patched, replaced with a composite as hard as bone. To obtain a tortoise, a person must first call the right state agency to fill out a permit. Then, a 150-square-foot escape-proof enclosure with hiding shelters, digging dirt, and watering holes must be created. The Desert Tortoise Adoption Committee will examine the proposed housing during a site visit, and if the hopeful applicant is approved, he or she will be in line to take care of an animal that is rather low maintenance: they hibernate for five months of the year.

Cheung, raised in Hong Kong until she was thirteen, always had a yearning for animals but was never allowed to have pets growing up. The backlash from her deprived childhood has allowed her to make up the thirteen years and more, having constructed a long history of companion animals that has culminated in the venerable Rose. She's followed a familiar route: Eugene the hamster, Kitty the cat (who was male, unbeknownst to Cheung at his christening). Guinness, Boomer, Wolfie—all shelter cats and dogs. A great saver of animals, Cheung confides that her family thinks she's crazy, but she would say it is her calling. After falling in love with the calm demeanor and novelty of desert tortoises, Cheung started down the ineluctable path toward being a provider. It took a year to construct what would become Rose's backyard habitat, and then it was time to do the formal adoption.

"They said they'd give us a smaller one, probably," she reminisces about the day she met Rose. The annex was filled with excited tension, participants pacing like nervous, new, expectant dads in delivery rooms. About two dozen tortoises were available for adoption, each boxed and ready, while the Adoption Committee official briefed each participant, filling out forms on an electronic tablet. Denise and her husband, Brad, received a quiet little box and carefully pulled back the cover to see Rose for the first time; the tortoise peered back at them with a look that was calm, caring, and inquisitive. It was love at first sight.

At home, Rose stayed still in her new home for about half an hour before beginning to explore. She was more adventurous than Denise and Brad had thought she would be, as the little tortoise jaunted through the pen and even tried to scale the perimeter walls.

It is the little things; one has to spend time with an animal to learn about its personality. Especially with nonmammalian animals. "Rose is self-sufficient . . . a wild animal. Why would she develop a relationship with a human the way a dog or cat does?" Cheung is matter-of-fact in her expectations, but I learn that just because a beast isn't cuddly doesn't mean that a person won't grow to love it. Rose may have been distant at first, but through time, Denise and Brad could call to her from the kitchen window and Rose would respond by raising her head. They've discovered that she's a picky eater sometimes but voracious on other occasions, wanting grape leaves to be removed from the vine before she'll consume the delicacy. She also plays, dismantling her dirt mound and then reconstructing it.

When Cheung sits in the garden that is Rose's abode, Rose will nudge at her human's toes, almost like a cat rubbing up against one's shin. "She'll nudge with her nose, but never bites."

The day of adoption, scanning the tortoise-filled boxes in the room, Cheung noticed that most of the crates were like Rose's, silent as if they held no more than air. One, however, was animated, banging and scuttling across the room. That tortoise in particular was slated for "someone with more experience." When a man Denise and Brad were talking to was presented the box, they peered inside to see a large male tortoise, intent on a jail break, staring down his new owner. Cheung, sighed, relieved. "I don't know if I could have handled that one." Indeed, perhaps that is why the Desert Tortoise Adoption booklet states the primary reason people adopt a tortoise is because, "just like people, tortoises have their own personality (but don't talk back)." For some tortoises, however, new versions of the guide may have to revise the talking back part.

As people spend time with individual animals, the individual behavioral traits become more evident. Adopting a desert tortoise may not have been the first place to go searching for personality, but there it was. There was a striking difference, even at first sight, between a tortoise that could be described as a *lover* growing to rub her chin on her protector's nose, and a *fighter* struggling to blast through his box, intimidating Cheung. Heart-warming stories aside, science must rise to the occasion too: tortoises have been around since the Permian Period, before dinosaurs.[15] They've survived the fragmenting of Pangea, multiple ice ages, a series of mass extinctions, and yet tortoises still thrive—so they must be doing something right. But why haven't all tortoises been honed sharply into a uniform epitome of chelonian perfection? Why do they vary?

In the chapters ahead, we'll examine the question of why evolution favors a variety of personalities within and among species. We'll survey a variety of ways that evolution has instilled similar personality types within widely disparate fauna. Animals are individuals, and if each individual were described wholly, there would be much accuracy but little understanding. Science looks for the patterns and understanding, not differences solely for the sake of identifying differences.

At first glance, one may think it most orderly to describe personality using a phylogenetic hierarchy—that is, from the "lowliest" of beings to the "higher" species. But we've already seen that chickens and tortoises may have as much personality as cats and dogs and dolphins, so the appropriate framework on which to study animal personality is not one that is organized on a phylogenetic tree. A better approach is grouping individual personalities *across* species by their similar evolutionary strategies. The personality tests described earlier provide a starting point for identifying the tendencies to look for when studying animal behavior, but they don't necessarily provide categories into which a wild animal is easily placed. And let's not forget that the animals being observed are in most cases roaming unfettered, and certainly lack the ability to answer a questionnaire. So, for our examination, we will discuss a variety of recognizable traits, but categorize them into continuums that have particular evolutionary relevance and intuitive definitions: brave fighter to serene lover, famished predator to cautious prey, herding to hermetic, and exploring wayfarer to homebound wallflower. From there, the patterns become apparent: on evolutionary terms, having a winning personality is as important as an animal's physiological adaptations.

CHAPTER 3

Brave Fighter
or Serene Lover

We found Celeste near a dumpster. Fluffy, quiet, and uncollared, with limpid blue eyes that crossed slightly, the sweet cat gladly adopted us and our house. She had peculiarities that set her apart from Pingüino. His lines were crisp black and white. She was long-haired and a mottled mutt of a cat. He was aggressive, pouncing on mice and birds and living on lizards, but Celeste stared blankly, like a beautiful model, fluffy and sweet with what seemed like very little activity between her ears. He preferred easing his paws down the bowls of toilets to drink, while she had a ritual of jumping into the kitchen sink every morning. She waited for me to stumble downstairs to make coffee. While it brewed, she had me leave the faucet slowly dripping so she could lick from the dribble like a hamster. Finished, she stared into space, and sometimes, the faucet left on, the water would drip onto her head and down the side of her back. I thought that, as a rule, cats hated water and would avoid a bath or spray at any cost, but Celeste didn't notice, didn't care. If it wasn't for the kindness of strangers, she certainly would have starved. She was a lover, not a fighter, and in our house she lived a wonderful life, with plenty of food, cool tap water, and gentle showers. In the cat neighborhood, however, the passive approach to life was not as rewarding.

Another cat on the block we considered the epitome of evil. As satanic cats often are, he was white, fluffy, and big-eyed adorable.

We named him Snowball. Pingüino was aggressive, a killer, but he had his limits. When Snowball came into the yard, Pingüino acquiesced, staying close to the house and out of reach. Instead of behaving like a predator, Pingüino focused on not being treated as prey. Celeste, as innocent, serene, and harmless as a mouse, unfortunately, would stroll unknowingly right into the jaws of hell. Snowball was agitated by Celeste's intrusion and would respond with force, descending upon the oblivious cat like a Valkyrie. The fight was short because Celeste did not know what to do besides cower and take a beating. Pingüino, being who he is, lounged on the deck flipping his tail, looking up to the sky and pretending not to notice. It was up to me to chase off Snowball, which I did whenever I saw him.

Celeste had a sweetness, a calmness, and an endearing cuddliness about her. She could be petted for long periods without indicating she was finished by turning and biting. She would follow us as we walked our elementary-school-aged son three blocks to school. She looped through the crosswalk past the adoring eyes of the crossing guard. Arriving at the steps of Adams Elementary, she'd look up, puzzled, completely lost. We'd carry her back home, late for work or not. Some animals are so much sweeter than others—like some little boys who read books while others throw rocks. Lovers, friends, pets, and children—we humans find ways to love them, each for the unique way they have adapted to the world.

Still, why are some individuals, like Snowball, so prone to fight? Doesn't he who lives by the sword, die by the sword? Is there strength in weakness or weakness in weakness? How can it be that two animals of the same species could be so fundamentally different? Celeste was the Blanche DuBois of the cat world, swallowed up by her own misunderstanding of the environment she found herself in. Pingüino was too likeable to be Stanley Kowalski, but he was similar in his aggressive charge at life. Celeste was satisfied by gentle caresses and leftovers, Snowball wanted to rule the neighborhood, and Pingüino would sneak away to eat the Bluebird of Happiness.

―――

Western bluebirds are idyllic serenity incarnate, with iridescent blue hues in bright sunlight. Orange-red breasts opposing their wings, neck, and head make the blue appear all the bluer. They flitter and dive for bugs, then disappear into cavities in trees. The breeding season is a time of frenetic activity as the males claim territories and chase away intruders. Bluebirds don't have the head-pounding proclivity of woodpeckers, but they do rely on the bug-foraging burrows of their avian brethren.[1] It's a reproductive challenge for the males, who can't attract a female unless they control a chunk of stable neighborhood. Location, location, location. They have to woo their mates with the right mix of foraging sites and nest holes.[2]

Other than requiring old forests with an ample supply of nest cavities, western bluebirds are somewhat flexible in how they live and what they eat; they have a fondness for berries, but also enjoy earthworms, snails, and other ground invertebrates.[3] Sometimes they will sit on lower branches and wait for insects to fly by, which they capture by "hawking," when they snatch bugs out of the air. They also fall from perches to dive bomb onto the invertebrates creeping and crawling on the ground.

The most desirable territories have the right mix of vegetation and plenty of perches where males can rest while scanning the ground for prey. Defending the territory is essential, and the birds' battles can be fierce. Females can be fickle, and competing males mischievous. Unless a male with a large territory is particularly vigilant, many of the hatchlings will not be his, the cuckold's tireless efforts spent on helping to raise another male's young. The male bluebird is a dedicated dad, actively fighting for his territory and mate. He feeds her while she's brooding, and then helps feed the chicks that hatch. To sum up, the symbol of happiness is actually an overworked dad with three jobs.

Renée Duckworth, an equally overworked researcher, wandered among the mosaic of open meadows and thick stands of Douglas firs and ponderosa pines that laid like a quilt over the Lolo National Forest in Montana. Her task was to search the trunks of mature trees and decaying snags for nest cavities that would be suitable nesting locations for bluebirds. Having found the holes, she added her own, placing standardized nest boxes next to the cavities. Conditions set, she controlled the density and quality of homes for brooding bluebirds in the wilds of western Montana. Research seems to flow in fits and starts, like the punctuated equilibrium of evolution, and just after finding and altering the nesting environment, she had to wait.

The next year she returned to the forest and began capturing bluebirds. Sometimes she'd lure the hungry birds to feeding platforms baited with mealworms or other times reach in to pull them from their nest boxes. With a bird in hand, she'd mark them with uniquely colored leg bands and measure their wings, legs, and tails. Knowing who was who and where they lived, the fun could begin. Much of Duckworth's brilliance was shown in her systematic approach to observation and experimentation with the innocent bluebirds' territorial behaviors. This she did mostly by pissing them off.

Beginning with the obvious, when Duckworth measured the males, she found that they varied physically, with some having majestically long tails and legs. So equipped, she supposed, in order to be swooping fliers, better at sailing through open spaces to nab insects on the wing. Other birds, like sleek and agile jet fighters with shorter wings and legs, she assumed would be better aerial acrobats in the more dense forest interior. If birds matched themselves to the particular right environment, she reasoned, then they'd be better fathers and produce more young.

Indeed, short-tailed males raised more offspring in dense vegetation and long-tailed animals raised more young when they established territories in the open areas. So, putting on Darwin's lenses, it should be obvious that long-tailed birds fight for territories in the open and prefer them, and short-tailed males prefer the opposite.

As happens so often in science, however, Duckworth determined that the obvious conclusion is not the case.[4] Physiology is readily apparent—long tails or short ones—but other important factors guide birds' choices too. Differences in personality of western bluebirds lead to different choices and ultimately affect natural selection even more than the physiological traits on which scientists have historically tended to focus.

One difficulty with measuring intangibles such as personality is that it can be exceedingly difficult to know individual animals in the wild. One usually has to have animals in captivity of some sort to do close observations, to measure behavioral traits. Duckworth, however, found clever ways to test western bluebirds outside captivity, and she focused on the birds' proclivity for aggression.

Western bluebirds depend on the holes in trees left by other species such as woodpeckers. It's the angry birds, the aggressive males who fight incessantly, who win the territories with the most nesting cavities. Therefore, the bellicose little birds will respond violently toward intruding conspecifics (individuals of the same species) and other cavity-nesting species that annoy them. Tree swallows, for instance, compete for nest locations and are as irritating to bluebirds as other bluebirds.

Duckworth returned to the verdant forests and fields of western Montana to find nest boxes filled with bluebird pairs preparing to start their families.[5] She carried with her little wire cages, like terrestrial versions of a shark cage, sized not for scuba divers but rather for tree swallows. Duckworth acknowledges the magnitude of the tasks the little birds have. "I personally favor the swallow. . . . They are like the scrappy little cousins, the underdog." Each tree swallow, safe it its protective cage, was installed within sight of the bluebird's nest (the cages' wires were too tight for the birds to physically contact or hurt each other, and all the vexed swallows were released safely after the experiments). Her research study involved moving from tree to tree, baiting each bird, and then sitting back to watch the fireworks from a nearby blind. Then, she counted the frequency of attacks as macho male bluebirds harassed the intruder. No one knows the intricacies of the bluebird soap opera more than Renée Duckworth. She'd be mildly annoyed to be pigeonholed into such a narrow description as an expert on bluebird behavior—she considers herself an evolutionary ecologist who uses bluebirds as a model—but the fact is that her work with the busy little birds is foundational.[6]

Aggressive fighters, she observed, were better at holding territories that had the most nesting cavities. But what about her earlier physiological observations? Males with big legs and tails that have more young when they homestead the open areas and males with shorter tails that raise more young when they create territories in dense vegetation? The twist in the story that Duckworth discovered was that the physiological aspect scientists most easily observe was not what determined the birds' choices.

Yes, aggressive males acquired territories with the most nest cavities, but they were blind with rage and fought to hold more land, but not necessarily the land to which they were most suited. Ironically, by fighting so hard, they ended up in places where they just weren't physically built to perform so well. They chose territories depending upon how aggressive they were instead of matching their body form to the best environment for them. Thus, their personality and not their physiology determined where they nested, and ultimately how successful they'd be as lovers and fathers.

I enjoy it when science aligns with what my mother told me growing up: personality is more important than looks.

So, if it is personality—more specifically, aggressiveness—that drives western bluebird society and reproduction, why do the birds still vary in personality? Such questions are at the heart of what drives Duckworth in her science, and she relates how her own personality developed and compelled her to do what she does. Growing up with "an acre of woods between two cornfields" in Ohio, she was drawn to the wonder of the natural world at an early age. She was also simultaneously attracted to psychology, and she proudly remembers a middle-school science project in which she answered the question "why do we dream?" Melding the two passions perfectly, she can be outside trying to peek into the heads of bluebirds and push the limits of the question "why?"

A fundamental why to Duckworth, which is also at the heart of this book, has to do with animal personality types in the context of natural selection. If we just determined that aggressive birds get bigger territories with more nest cavities, why are there still peaceniks among them? The answer is in the balanced interplay between being a fighter or a lover and the environment. Duckworth's angry birds often sacrificed living in habitat better suited to them for owning more habitat and nest cavities. Also, males that spent the most time fighting couldn't use that time for foraging and feeding their mates. If the females have to leave the eggs to feed instead of incubating them, their chicks' chances of survival are reduced. Being aggressive means bigger territories with more nesting options, but being passive means more time to gather rather than fight.

Duckworth determined that the lovebirds, being more able, male and female, to dote on their young, were better at producing fledglings. Again, thinking about natural selection, that's the golden ring: those traits that allow an animal to survive and reproduce successfully are passed on. "Why" Duckworth asked, "do the fighters fight so much when they lose out by not being able to successfully raise young?" What is the benefit of being more a fighter than a lover?

———

"Some are born great, some achieve greatness, and some have greatness thrust upon them" is one of my favorite Shakespeare lines, although it drips with irony as Malvolio speaks. Several times in *Twelfth Night*, the Bard asks a question that is germane to a discussion about individuals within populations: What type of person rises to the heights within a social order?

Certainly bluebirds have more aggressive animals that dominate patches, but other species, such as mountain chickadees (*Poecile gambeli*), have individuals that rise in dominance through their strength of will. Dominance is important for the little birds, as the higher ranking males have higher potential for survival and reproduction.

Rebecca Fox, at the University of Nevada, Reno, wanted to know what types of chickadees rose within the social ranks.[7] Is it the brave and aggressive birds that dominate? Assuming that birds that were braver or confident in novel environments would win in social competition with other birds, Fox and her colleagues made their observations. They captured forty-eight birds from the wild and brought their subjects back to live in individual cages for a few weeks. To measure a bird's tendency toward exploration, the researchers opened each bird's cage to a larger room with several perches in it. The timorous birds would remain in or near their cage. The brave birds would flitter from perch to perch throughout the room. An added challenge to intimidate the little chickadees, the scientists hung a plastic Pink Panther key chain from the perch (I loved that they provided that level of detail in their paper). Particularly brave and bold birds would approach and peck at the novel object, and shy birds would not land on the perch it was hung from.

How did personality type influence where a bird established itself in a pecking order? After determining each bird's personality type on the brave and aggressive continuums, the researchers then paired them up in the large room again and observed which bird was dominant over the others. Dominance is expressed in two ways in chickadees: dominant birds will actively attack others, but subordinate birds will also proactively move away from prime perches, yielding them to a higher ranking bird.

The results were intriguing. The researchers did not find a strong personality type in a bird's willingness to investigate a novel object. The birds did not sort into strong groups but distributed across the continuum. How brave they were in that context also didn't translate to how dominant they were over their fellow birds. The researchers did find, however, that how confident and brave birds were in launching out into a novel environment was a defined and significant personality type. The birds either bravely launched into the new room or timidly avoided it. Were the brave animals the most dominant? In short, no. In ten of twelve pairings between brave and timid, the less adventurous bird became dominant; homebodies were significantly more likely to rule the roost.

The research is a reminder not to fall fool to fallible interpretations, as Malvolio did, but to think through the evidence regarding personality and be aware of potential pitfalls. The first of which is the meaning of terms. I use terms such as *brave*, and researchers frequently use terms such as *bold*, but the words themselves can have drastically different meanings. The other pitfall is context, as Fox's investigation highlighted. A bird may be bold and brave in a novel environment but also cowardly and henpecked in another.

In my garden, I found an orb-web spider, a yellow and black jewel set in strands of gossamer filaments. I paused, studying distinct boundaries of the two tones. My mind succumbed to the beast's abstract cloak, painted like Rorschach's diversion. The splash of bright color dabbed on obsidian is what first caught my eye, but when she moved I saw that she was not a garden stone but a virile dancer. Her adorned body was not her only defining attribute. Tall, black, go-go like boots rose from her feet, leaving exposed the tan above her knees. Her legs moved gracefully across her stage like fingers sweeping scales over piano keys. I fear that too often, for art and for science, people are oblivious to beauty, to wonder, to the depths of capabilities of life.

Do we expect such beauty in an everyday garden? Is our sin one of ignoring or denying, or are our biases so ingrained that we cannot think of a thing such as an orb-web spider as having beauty, behavior, and individuality? She is as industrious as she is beautiful, spinning a web each morning only to consume it and reweave the following day. It shouldn't be any wonder that her beaus are smitten to the point of peril.

Some scientists, as prurient as the rest of us, find the courting and mating system of the orb-web spider (*Argiope aurantia*) particularly intriguing. These spiders, like the *Hilara* flies, engage in acts of bizarre behavior—sexual cannibalism. Two pioneering researchers, Kapil K. Khadka and Matthias W. Foellmer, created colonies of spiders like entomological zoological gardens filled with dancing jewels. The spiders may not be the first species we'd consider to learn about animal personality, but given the interplay between sex and death in their social systems, they are perfect candidates for learning about trends in aggressiveness, loving, and fighting in the animal world.

Khadka and Foellmer started with cute juvenile "spiderlings" who were reared together in terraria. The researchers constructed chicken-wire frames so that the baby spiders would have structures to build webs on. They then let fruit flies fly freely—into the spiderlings' silk. When the juvenile females were large enough, Foellmer and Khadka pampered each potential mother with mealworm larvae dinners and then gave each spiderling her own acrylic box to live in. The small-statured males got a tiny plastic vial for a home.

The games would soon heat up, however, as the spiders spiced the drama in their lives with violent sex. The act is culminated, as with any species, by the transfer of sperm. In orb-web spiders, a male uses two inflatable organs, called pedipalps, for the task, which he inserts into the female's genitalia. Unfortunately for the males, most females (about 80 percent) attack males within one second of insertion of the first pedipalp. The females are about fifty times heavier than the males, so perhaps it is no trouble for her to make her suitors her snacks. Some females, however, are less playful with their mates than others, and after attacking, about 25 percent of the females kill their suitors before the males can insert their second copulatory organ and fully complete the deed.[8]

Khadka and Foellmer asked, was there something in particular about individual female spiders that caused their proclivity to kill their mates? To answer the question, the researchers measured aggressiveness in each spider as both a juvenile and an adult by dropping a cricket into her web and recording the amount of time she took to attack the prey. Because size and condition could have effects the researchers needed to know about, they also measured body size of the females. How did they measure the leggy subjects? Commonplace for researchers, they dropped the spiders into a vial of CO_2, which anesthetizes them long enough for the researchers to take body measurements.

Knowing how aggressive each of their subject females were with crickets, the researchers measured the females' hunger in a sexual context. They first fed the females mealworm larvae the day before the experimental trial so they wouldn't be famished. Then the researchers gently placed randomly chosen males onto a female's web and waited for him to court, and for her to decide. The trials had a simple, dichotomous outcome: the female killed her suitor or she didn't.

From their testing the researchers found that there were different types of females varying in degrees of aggressiveness. About 20 percent of the females they observed didn't attack their mates, 60 percent attacked with lackluster animosity and didn't kill the males, and 20 percent of the mounting males met their doom before they could fully copulate. Was it something innate or demonstrable earlier in life that could explain the viciousness of the deadliest females?

Was there some personality trait such that the fiercest predators were just aggressive in general and the behavior spilled over into the sexual act? There were other hypotheses that the researchers needed to rule out too: killing mates may not have been a personality trait but just a result of a female being relatively small and really, really hungry.

Did size matter? Size of male? Size of female? Difference in size between them? In short, no. None of the physiological measurements were correlated with outcome of the sexual encounter. Behavior, especially how aggressively predatory the females were when young, did correlate with their aggression toward males. The relationship wasn't perfect, however, and only about 21 percent of the sexual attacks were statistically explained by a female spider's aggressiveness toward crickets. A distinct group of females that were timid around crickets when young were aggressive around males and killed their mates. The research showed that even in spiders there is a range of individuals, some more aggressive than others, with more aggressive tendencies in different contexts, but not all spiders behave equally in all situations.

Aric W. Berning and a slew of coauthors worked with the funnel-web spider *Agelenopsis pennsylvanica* to better understand traits of female spiders.[9] In experiments similar to Khadka and Foellmer's, Berning's assistants also measured aggressiveness toward prey by dropping little crickets into the female's lair and measuring how long it took for the predator to attack. After learning how aggressive each huntress was, they introduced the males.

Some females were voracious, moving on prey with celerity. Others were less so, biding time before attacking. Repeating measurements on individuals, and not just among individuals, the researchers also reported in their dry language that attack scores were "highly repeatable." Although some spiders were more aggressive than others, the researchers could cleverly manufacture aggressiveness in any spider by withholding food. (Sort of a no-brainer for anyone who's gotten cranky on an empty stomach.) Ultimately, two measurements best predicted the fate of a mating male during the mating trials: whether or not the female had a high-prey drive around crickets, and whether or not she was hungry.

Personality can be described as ENTJ, or as fighter or lover, but it is important to remember that labels describe a trend within an individual and not an invariant measurement. A person, for example, who has had a bad day at the office, had a terrible commute, and stubbed his toe on the way in the door may snap and cuss at a colleague one morning. Does that make him a bitter and angry person? Not necessarily. The point is that humans are not unique in the way our individual personalities vary with time and circumstance. Even spiders can get hungry and grumpy and act out of character. Berning and his coauthors pointed out that "the danger of attempting courtship with a given female is both a function of her innate behavioural tendencies and her recent feeding history."[10] The most successful males not only had to first find the nice spiders but also had to find them when they were in a good mood.

———

Another tiny dancer, a fishing spider (*Dolomedes spp*), waits in the shallows for arthropods that drop onto the water surface. It gets worse for an unlucky bug, who is already experiencing the misfortune of falling into water when a fishing spider attacks. Adept hunters, fishing spiders do not limit their fare to helpless derelicts; they also enjoy small fish and tadpoles. Another favorite meal of the female fishing spiders, as one might expect, is male fishing spiders. Such a delicacy the males are that the cannibalistic tendency effects changes in local populations. Males hatch first, and then females, and when all the spiderlings are first exploring their worlds, the sex ratio is fifty-fifty. Shortly after females hatch, however, the sex ratio skews and male numbers are measurably diminished due to female dinners.

Courtship encounters obviously have particular importance for males, and in the wondrous process of natural selection, they have developed a ritualized mating dance. The males wave their legs and vibrate the females' webs to put the females in the mood. After the dance, the males approach nervously. If she has not been soothed by his dance, he could become lunch.

Swedish researchers Göran Arnqvist and Stefan Henriksson collected sixty female and fifty-five male spiders from wet meadows next to the Vindalälven River and gave the spiders posh new aquarium homes furnished with water and Styrofoam floats to relax on.[11] The researchers wanted to know why, if the goal is to reproduce, females would eat the males before copulation was complete, risking the fertility of their eggs.

In another example of soap opera as scientific experiment, Arnqvist and Henriksson placed males into a female's aquarium and allowed them to interact for forty-five minutes—if they survived. The odds weren't great, as the researchers determined that in 78 percent of encounters, the females would pursue and attack the courting males. It is a mating system much riskier for males than buying a woman a drink at a fern bar. Happily for the male spiders, however, most escaped, and only 11 percent of the attacked males were killed and eaten. Some lucky males found calm females and were allowed to mount them, but only 22 percent of the time. It typically takes only a few seconds to insert each pedipalp and to transfer sperm, but postcoital cuddling and bliss is lacking as the male must unromantically jump free and run away, literally, for his life.

After the females laid their egg sacs and nursed them for ten days, the evolutionary significance of the differences in female behavior were readily apparent. The average fertilization rates of females that received only one male papal insertion was only 35 percent; if they tolerated both pedipalps, 97 percent were fertile. Virgin females, of course, laid only unfertilized eggs, thus ending their line. The aggressive females, overcome by their literal hunger for males, essentially sterilized themselves.

How could this be? If aggressive females can't reproduce, why are there still aggressive females? The theme of behavioral variability, and evolution's demand for it even when some behaviors are counterintuitive, is one we will return to repeatedly in this book. For fishing spiders, the answer is that the number of eggs a female can lay is a product of how much food she eats when young. Which is a product of how aggressive a hunter she is. Being bigger is a good thing for a female spider, because her large and healthy body can create more eggs. But being a small and prolific lover has its benefits too; although she may not lay as many eggs, they will all be fertilized. Being either type of spider has advantages, to a point, so nature chooses both.

———

Another species that has to choose between fighting and loving may be more well-known to us than spiders. Water striders are especially familiar to children playing beside standing pools of water, throwing pebbles into ponds, and watching the creatures miraculously slide across the surface. Their legs, covered with water repelling hairs, suspend them on the water's surface. They kick into the water and propel themselves off of imperceptible vortices they create.[12] Other bugs that fall on the surface can't propel themselves and are easy prey to the predatory water walkers.

Andrew Sih is most definitely Mr. Personality, not only for his own amiable traits but also because his work has been at the forefront of animal personality research. Sih has been studying predator and prey relationships at the University of California, Davis, for decades.

In a long line of papers, Andrew Sih examined individuality in water striders and how the individuals have different approaches to life.[13] Some species are easier to collect than others. To find their subjects, Sih and his colleagues only had to traipse over to a stream on the UC Davis campus. They captured their striders, then labeled each one with a unique colored paint mark and kept them in a series of kid-sized pools, separated by riffles, for observations. They observed a group of fifty animals each day, half males and half females. They recorded each individual's preference for remaining still in the pools or darting through the riffles, and for staying near the edges and cover or venturing out in the open. They tracked how each strider moved or rested, ate or mated. The scientists also examined how the striders interacted with each other: whether each strider chased, struggled, or jumped on another strider.

It was immediately apparent that some striders were, for lack of a better word, the passive, lazy ones. Others were go-getters, moving about much more. Another facet of each was how aggressive they were, chasing and fighting or leaving each other alone. Using a statistical procedure called a principle components analysis, the researchers combined all the measurements for each individual and created a mathematical continuum, with several factors, that described each individual. On one end of the continuum males were lethargic and peaceful, but on the other they were active, aggressive fighters.

The next step that Sih made was the thing I find the most fun about science. Great scientists don't stop with an observation, such as some striders are aggressive and some are lazy. Sih and his colleagues pushed on asking, what if? They tweaked the system, messing with the little striders in ways similar to how Duckworth taunted bluebirds. Sih separated individual striders into groups based on strider personality. They created some groups of males by picking out the listless ones and grouping them, and then constructed other groups of the animated animals. Which ones faired best in the pools?

Sih and his colleagues first needed to demonstrate that the way the striders acted wasn't just because of the environment where they were initially living. They had to rule out the notion that the lethargic males who rested on the sides of pools weren't just browbeaten into it. The scientist wanted to determine if internal or external conditions determined where the striders chose to be. Would the same animal, put into a different situation, retain the same personality traits? If it didn't, the strider was stimulus-response, with no actual evidence of personality. So they grouped some fighters with fighters, fighters with passive striders, and passive striders together to see what would happen.

As we've seen previously, the animals were indeed consistent in how they acted before and after they were grouped and regrouped. It wasn't that the inactive animals were just henpecked to the sides of their original pools. It was inherent in how each animal acted, whether they were surrounded by other slow males or by aggressive ones. At least that was true in general. Sih and his colleagues also observed a few examples of certain animals being invigorated by new surroundings; one lethargic male became hyperaggressive when grouped with other mellow males. Even similar water striders are not the same. They make their own rules.

How do the different personality types play out relative to natural selection? It seems that another recurring theme is sex. It all comes down to successful sex. When the researchers examined the love life of the striders, they identified a system with a trade-off much like that for bluebirds. Water striders are not the most romantic of species. Essentially, the males jump on another strider they see pass by. If it is a male, they'll usually jump off. If it is a female, they'll try desperately to mate with her, as she tries equally hard to knock him off and escape. Females, expert gymnasts, avoid the males' genital connection by doing a series of backward summersaults to dislodge them.[14] In this strategy of forced copulation, the researchers expected that when they mixed it up and put groups of males with females, there would be a strong correlation; that in this system the aggressive fighters would outcompete the passive lovers. But the correlation, first observed, wasn't strong.

Peering more closely, researchers saw that male energy and swagger was effective for mating, but only to a point. To compare it to humans, I think of activity and confidence in human males as attributes that may normally be attractive to potential mates, but only up to the point of someone being overly assertive—what is often referred to in technical language as an asshole. So it is with water striders. Certain males whom Sih and colleagues observed were so hyperaggressive they actually drove females to flee from the pools the males inhabited. The females remained in the pools with the more passive males, who didn't jump on them as much but also didn't scare them away and with whom they'd eventually mate.

Once again, the evidence is that, in any given circumstance, nature prefers particular traits or personalities over others. Over time, however, due to constantly changing conditions, nature demands that a species retain plasticity and variation in personality types.

Female choice interacts with male personality in many other species too. Consider the broad-horned flour beetle (*Gnatocerus cornutus*).[15] This is not a species that I am as easily able to wax poetic about. Males of the species resemble long, segmented potatoes with legs. Their most defining features are their large mandibles that extend like scimitars and include the structural detail of cross-guards formed from a fold of armor at the mandible's base. Indeed, flour beetles are built to fight, and they use their oversized mouthparts to wrestle with other males.

Fighting allows individuals to win over and banish rivals. The stronger and more aggressive victors then presumably have more access to females. Not only that, but it has long been proposed that the most powerful males, by out-competing their competitors, prove themselves more worthy and are more attractive to females. Or are they? Which was the point of a study by a cobble of researchers from Okayama University, Japan; the University of Tsukuba, Japan; and the University of Exeter, United Kingdom, led by Kensuke Okada, who looked at the specifics of such an idea by observing broad-horned flour beetles.[16]

To determine which males were most attractive, the researchers determined who mated with whom. They dropped females into a dish, and then put a male in with them. Male beetles have a courting dance they use to gain the females' favors. The male positions himself behind the female and then mounts her and taps her back while rubbing her body with his. If his massage is worthy, the female extends her egg-laying ovipositor and after a short genital coupling, the two are mated. The researchers used the trials, determining courtship quantity and quality by measuring how receptive females were to individual males. Essentially, the better the males stroked and courted the females, the more successful they were at mating.

Even lowly beetles have something to teach scientists about questioning our previous assumptions about the importance of physiology over behavior. The accepted theory about flour beetles was that the males with the big mandibles would win the fights and be more attractive to females, due to their masculine size and fighting prowess. Kensuke Okada and colleagues, however, determined that there was no relationship between the size of a beetle's mandible and his sexiness. The adage about the "size of the ship" being less important in intimate relationships than the "motion in the ocean" holds true experimentally, even for beetles.

The trade-off, it appears, has to do with the interplay between genetics, physiology, and personality. In beetle romance, aggressive males will usually have more access to females by displacing other males. The females, however, take a risk in that the more masculine males will produce more masculine females that are less fecund. The lovers, then, are favored for that characteristic, and the variability they introduce provides balance to the population.

———

Sleepy lizards (*Tiliqua rugosa*) in South Australia are not actually all that lethargic. They are magnificent little beasts, cute in a crocodilian sort of way, with short and stubby tails and laterally jutting undersized legs. They are the Pembroke Welsh corgi of the reptile world. Their little toes splay as they stand their ground on the desert sand and bravely resist a potential predator by ferociously gaping their large mouth and wagging a hideous blue tongue. They appear to be able to back up their intrepidity too, the armor of their broad scales giving them the alternate appellation of shingle-back lizard.

The animals have work to do, as we all do, and fortunately for them, much of their effort is associated with socializing, mating, and reproduction. They are relatively large and long-lived lizards that reside together, with overlapping home ranges. The males and females form pair bonds each spring, cavorting together for more than two months before they mate. They often reunite every year, but not always, and the strength of the pair bond can vary. As indicated by the title of the chapter, male sleepy lizards, like the other species discussed, can be aggressive toward each other. Their battles can lead to significant injury.[17]

Stephanie Godfrey, along with her colleagues, including Andrew Sih, "investigated whether intraspecific variation in aggressiveness among individual male lizards influenced their associations with other lizards, and whether we could identify a behavioural syndrome linking aggressiveness and social network position."[18] That is, they observed different personality types in male lizards and determined what influence they had in their lizard society.

The authors captured sixty adult lizards and, using surgical tape, attached GPS data loggers to the top of their tails. The monitors recorded the lizards' locations every ten minutes. Summarizing the data, the scientists knew where the lizards were, but more important, they documented who was hanging out with whom. They used two methods to determine how much of a fighter each male was. The first was simple: when the researchers recaptured the males every two weeks, they counted each lizard's new scale damage from fighting. The second was more like the teasing of bluebirds. The researchers dangled a threatening-looking model in front of each lizard subject. It was a simple matter to rank the males' responses to the intruder on a scale of one (not aggressive) to eleven (very aggressive). Eleven, being one more than ten, denotes a particularly aggressive tendency, as observed by previous practitioners.[19]

When the results were in, Godfrey and colleagues determined that some lizards were lovers. Not only were they less aggressive but they also were more strongly connected with the females that they associated with. The fighters were more aggressive and spent less time with their partners, similar to bluebird society. Sometimes males focus on fighting so much that although they may win all their fights, they don't have enough time afterward to successfully court a female that season.

Even lizards, living in little societies, have to find the balance between dominance over others and attractiveness to mates. How can aggressive males remain in the population if they don't reproduce? It may have something to do with social status and fighting their way to the top of lizard hierarchy. There are lizards who, rather than be great lovers when young, are scrappy and domineering at first, and then like elder statesmen calm down and reap the benefits during their dotage.

In high-school civics lessons, students may discuss how human societies, especially those conglomerated into countries, should comport themselves. Which do we choose, guns or butter? Do we keep our country safe and cohesive by putting resources into a large and active military, taking the fighter approach? Or do we focus on compassionate cooperation, feeding the poor, choosing to be lovers to our brothers and sisters first?

In response, I again propose zoomorphizing, using animals and their behaviors and societies as mirrors of human individual and collective behaviors. Lovers or fighters? We can turn to the animals for expectations, if not absolute answers, too.

Humans are not that different from spiders, striders, and bluebirds, and indeed, there is likely considerable benefit in using a comparative approach to examine animal personalities and societies in the light of human ones. Our national economies operate under the same pressures that produce passive Celeste, aggressive Snowball, and passive-aggressive Pingüino. There are pressures that keep bluebirds fighting, female spiders attacking and eating males, and water striders harassing away their potential mates. Simultaneously, there are pressures that make some bluebirds the most attentive fathers, some spiders with more will to love than to kill, and some striders more successful by being nerdy wallflowers. There are dominant flour beetles who try to exclude the males that the females find more attractive.

Humans can learn much from animals, so similar they are in temperament to ourselves and our societies. I can't help but apply what I've learned about animal personalities to the human world. Nature's love for variety makes me think that aggressors and war will always exist, but if we see our similarities with the animals, perhaps we'll be able to better understand why we are the way we are and be cognizant of our foibles. It's not a passing philosophical notion either—balancing our bellicose propensities with our peaceful ones—because humanity has perfected our weapons to the point that we can cause our own extinction. Having too many serene lovers may seem like it would usher in an age of unambitious ennui, but one too many brave fighters who are willing to push to the brink of nuclear war will spawn an age of doom.

CHAPTER 4

Appetite or Appetizer

Pingüino really should stay inside. It would be the right thing to do and would rescue me from hypocrisy and embarrassment as I, a wildlife biologist, have an indoor-outdoor cat. A cat that can grow fat on kibble while mercilessly killing beautiful birds for fun. He demands the opportunity to express himself as a blood-thirsty killer, significantly different from my neighbors' indoor cats who have to limit their predatory instincts to incomplete attacks on feather dusters. Pingüino cries to go out, and then wanders the neighborhood with haughty disregard to the Wildlife Society's impugning.

I tell myself that Pingüino *earned* his freedom. During our travels together, the dude has been potential fodder for everything from hawks to coyotes to cars, especially during the time he spent lost in the wilderness. Doesn't he deserve, I rationalize, a little time as the predator that he is?

It's particularly poignant when I think of Pingüino's natural rival, the famous cat killer of southern California, the coyote. Coyotes have a similar standing in the wild. Mighty hunters in some ways, they are susceptible to a variety of early and bloody deaths: killed by intolerant wolves, smacked by bears, ambushed by cougars, squashed by a speeding car, or shot by a camouflaged hunter. Coyotes survive within the interstices between predator and prey, between blood and roughage. Some coyotes are ravenous hunters of rabbits, mice, and deer; they live by the sharpness of their canines. I've spent hours watching them in the Lamar landscape of Yellowstone. Usually they are efficient killers, but also I've seen them pounce and play with mice, flinging one into the air playfully and pouncing and throwing repeatedly while the rodent squeaks and struggles. Is it sick that they love to hunt and that they play with their food? In contrast, some coyotes survive on berries and crickets and are loathsome to farmers as predators on watermelon. Is a coyote or a cat a predator or prey? Is the nature of a species determined by what it eats, its drive to kill or forage, or by what will eat it?

My acceptance of the existence of personality in a profusion of species, and using zoomorphizing as a mirror to understand human beings, did not come about as an epiphany, a eureka moment of clarity. Some of my first notions grew in the harsh environs of field research. I was working in Yellowstone National Park on January 17, 1991, tempting coyotes to fight over frozen carcasses at the edges of their territories. I saw such a strong parallel between us and them even then: coyotes formed sorties of hungry individuals that flew across invisible lines like the fighter pilots of Desert Storm. The hot desert sands of the first Gulf War were nothing like the powdery snow of a Wyoming winter. Still, observing coyotes, like soldiers, attempting to acquire a resource without dying while trying, played out on the ice before me and chilled me to the bone.

The coyotes had each other to fear as much as the bitter cold of winter in the Lamar Valley. I felt safe from them, but not from the environment. Below minus ten Fahrenheit, the cold there doesn't seep into your sleeves; it cracks into your clothing. The snow I walked across, leaving my winter quarters in the bunkhouse at Tower Junction, felt like walking on pure white talc. It was in sharp contrast to the slippery slush I know from my youth in coastal Alaska or during family holiday visits to Northern Virginia.

In my twenties, life was about excitement and adventure, and I welcomed the bitter wind biting at my cheek. It may have been a sting of pain, but I knew it as an exhilarating pinch of being alive. I reveled in nature's challenges, letting the wilderness build my character. Living alone in the Tower bunkhouse, doing radio tracking and scat collection surveys by myself, I was becoming accustomed to being alone. Although I'd enjoy time with friends and colleagues, I also found myself seeking out the unique thrill and exhilaration of achieving accomplishments alone.

Dragging a road-killed deer into a snow-covered meadow, for instance, I felt like I was a sled dog, researcher, and piece of the equation of life and death all rolled into one. Indeed, I suppose I was. I lucked into my position at Yellowstone, studying the coyotes of Lamar Valley and the adjoining lands even before the wolves arrived.

As I observed the other animals, my human fragility was not lost on me. Yellowstone is famous for winter denizens, such as the bison that shrug off blizzards and root into the drifts for morsels of dried vegetation without noticing the frost on their beards. Nature could have delivered me, along with the former deer at my feet, as fodder for the grizzlies in spring, but in the winter, insulated with down, sealed from head to toe as if ready for a Mars mission, I, a pathetic human, was the representation of the top predator. My technology allowed me to transcend the world where I lived, and I used it to observe a wild predator, clothed only in his own fur, somehow keeping naked paws from freezing on the ice and snow.

I struggled with the lifeless doe to bring her to the edge of two territories, an invisible boundary to my human senses. The technology of plotted map points from radio-marked coyotes again allowed me to discern a line that was lit in biological neon for the coyotes. I was a young researcher, my intellectual synapses strengthening. I wanted to learn how coyotes established their societies, built their virtual walls, and determine when they'd love, or fight, each other.

On a crisp night in winter, Yellowstone skies are brilliantly clear, a refulgent moon surrounded by scintillating stars. When the moon rests the white world goes dark, but the valleys of Yellowstone remain alive, bustling with predator and prey. I switched on my night vision goggles and the lightless valley became bright day, but all in shades of green. I looked to the sky, and every point of light was magnified, amplified into a cosmos of emerald infinities.

After hours of waiting, the lord of field mice, conqueror of carcasses, the coyote, finally came. It wasn't as if the animal pranced in like the mayor but rather it sulked timidly. I was amused by his hesitancy, his starts and sheepish retreats. It took an hour of approaching, scanning, retreating, and then returning to inch closer each time. The glorious calories of meat and entrails before it, I expected the little *Canis latrans* to rush in. A carnivore, sharpened canines—what could it be afraid of? The bears asleep, there were few things that would harm the animal. Because coyotes were protected in the park, I was only a symbol of danger, as humans would not shoot at him. Mountain lions can be threats, ambushing unwary coyotes who try to steal bites of the cat's stashed prey. Perhaps the smell of human and threat of cat caused the little predator pause. The coyote I watched for hours could not boldly rush in because he existed in the narrow space between predator and prey. He could always be the predator pouncing on field mice, but his feasts could end with a cougar's ambush. He intuitively knew that the event of eating punctuates two existences, a connection of one's death to another's life, like commas in a run-on sentence. Being eaten, of course, is the period at the end of the paragraph.

Observing coyotes long enough, I've concluded that they are bipolar animals: sometimes aggressive predators and sometimes wary cowards. The data and science support the conclusion, and people in addition to lonely field biologists scanning snow-covered fields are having the opportunity to see for themselves. Coyotes are rapidly becoming ubiquitous in suburban neighbors and can be found living in city parks too. As a result, coyote attacks on pets in suburban California have been on the increase, from 17 to 281 incidents from 1991 to 2003, about a 30 percent increase per year. Attacks on pets in Texas rose fourfold during the decade before 2003. Other, older, Canadian data from the Vancouver Ministry of Environment, Lands, and Parks documented a 315 percent increase in coyote complaints during a ten year span ending in 1995.[1] There were even 89 attacks on people between 1978 and 2003 in California. Press reports continue to describe attacks and conflicts, but given estimates of as many millions of coyotes scattered across North America, what are the real odds? That coyotes are predators is undisputed, but are all coyotes equally bold and bloodthirsty?

The idea of animal personality is relevant in human relations with other species on the planet, especially with the predatory ones.[2] There are millions of coyotes and many other large predators throughout America's vast landscape, but attacks by bears, wolves, or coyotes are actually rather rare given the overlap of animal activities and short-toothed, clawless, and pathetically defenseless human bodies. All animals could attack, but only some actually do. Why does one animal become an attacker of humans and others not? Certainly coyotes can learn to be less wary of us, to become habituated to our presence, but is there something else?

When Patrick Darrow, a student at Utah State University, began his investigation to examine how well a motion-activated device frightened away coyotes, he didn't know he'd end up discovering much more. Fortunate to be able to work at the Predator Research Facility in Millville, Utah, Darrow had access to a captive population of about one hundred coyotes in outdoor research pens. He was able to identify individuals and to tease out the differences in personality among them. Darrow trudged to each pen, carrying the speakers, light box, and motion detector. He carried hot dogs, too, but they weren't for his dinner. They were for the coyotes. Darrow turned on the motion-activated scare device, put out hot-dog baits behind it, and tracked how long it took for a coyote to rush past the device and eat the hot dogs. Night after night, he tracked which coyotes were undaunted by the lights and sounds so that he could determine which ones were bold and aggressive enough to dash through the hot dog's defenses. He expected what we've been taught to expect: a bell-shaped curve of responses with most lumping around the average in the middle, with rare extremes tailing off to either side. To Darrow's surprise, however, grouping the responses did not produce a normal curve. Instead, he found that there were different types of coyotes with different strategies for finding food, or avoiding becoming food.

There were the wary ones, a group of eight who were terrified by Darrow's electronic device. They gave up trying to approach and never ate the hot dogs. Three other pairs were the opposite: aggressive hunters who activated the devices more than 110 times each and boldly ate the treats in their first trial. They simply did not care about the "frightening" device. The group that was the most interesting, however, was composed of four coyote pairs that lived in the interstices: more than pusillanimous prey and less than rapacious predator. Initially these coyotes were frightened by the device and ran, but what was unique is that they didn't give up. They tried to get the hot dogs another time and another, but kept being repelled by the device. Eventually, however, they learned that the lights and sounds of Darrow's device were actually harmless. This group of coyotes persisted until they overcame their fear of the device, ignored it, and ate the hot dog treats.

Thus, the different coyotes had different behavioral strategies regarding food. They didn't fall into only aggressive predator or passive prey personalities. At a minimum, at least three types of coyotes fell within the predator-prey continuum.

Are coyotes unique in their partitioning of personalities? Coyotes are of modest size relative to other North American predators, usually weighing in at twenty to thirty pounds. They are big enough to lord over prey such as mice, voles, and rabbits, but they are small enough to be wimpy snacks for bears, wolves, and cougars. Are species such as wolves and bears, at the top of the food web, more uniform in their behavior because they can sneer down from the top of the predatory pyramid?

Humans have established a complicated bond with wolves; we've created a symbol much bigger than the species itself. Some humans have a long-standing hatred of the species; these fighters among us have traditionally dominated the human-wolf relationship. Evidence is in the historic actions that led to the extirpation of wolf populations. Today, however, the lovers of wolves are growing in number, as are wolf populations with them. But the potential for interactions between us is rising again.

It's exceptionally rare for a wolf to attack a person, and until the 1990s, there weren't any documented reports of healthy wolves killing people in the contiguous United States. The statistic is a bit disingenuous, because wolves had been almost entirely wiped out in the contiguous United States by the 1950s; since there haven't been wolves, there hasn't been any threat of an attack for more than five decades. One has to be a bit cautious when comparing conclusions about seldom-seen wolves to ubiquitous coyotes, but reports that we do have about lupine aggression toward humans are worth a look.

Looking back far and wide enough, it is clear that wolves do attack and kill humans.[3] Twelve children were reportedly killed in Holland in 1810 and 1811. The Beast of Gévaudan was blamed with killing more than 64 people in south central France in the mid-1700s. Wolves killed 136 people in Vimianzo, Spain, as recently as the mid-1950s. Wolves remain a threat to children in India, killing at least 88 children there in the mid-1990s. The broadly brushed accounts of historical wolf attacks in Europe, however, are not fine-grained enough. More recently, in North America, a thirty-two-year-old was killed by wolves in 2010 and a wolf attacked a person in Manitoba, Canada, in March 2013. These statistics tell a tale that should be blatantly obvious: duh, wolves are predators.

Examining the topic in more detail, Mark McNay investigated eighty reports of wolves fearlessly interacting with humans in Alaska and Canada.[4] He was largely interested in the explanation of sick or rabid wolves as being abnormal enough to attack. The nature of the encounters varied, however, and evidence for the sickly hypothesis did not build. McNay determined that in most of the cases the aggressive and fearless wolves were healthy. Wolves had, or were suspected of having, rabies in only 15 percent of the encounters. More specifically, the bold wolves came in two versions, thirty-nine (49 percent) wolves were aggressive and predatory toward humans, but twenty-nine (36 percent) were not aggressive but also not fearful. No one died, but in the eighty close interactions reported, there were sixteen bites. In that there are reliable reports of wolves attacking people, it is undeniable that there are aggressive, predatory wolves in the populations. But there are also curious ones who aren't overly aggressive, but who do persistently investigate potential prey. The shy ones don't show up in the statistics. Wolves are indeed predators, but because the hunger for human flesh is rare in their populations, it took centuries to accrue the wolf-attack tally. It wasn't that Little Red Riding Hood lied, but she certainly missed some of the finer points.

Bearded, rugged, loquacious, Nate Lance strung lines of nylon rope and red streaming flags across a research pen.[5] His concoction, *fladry*, was an old technique borrowed from the kingly days of Eastern Europe, when huntsmen would string rope festooned with strips of fabric in the forest. Wolves, when encountering the fladry, treated it as if it were a solid barrier and usually refused to cross. The concept has received a fair amount of modern attention for its potential for preventing conflicts between wolves and livestock. Using fifteen wolf packs in his experiment, Lance tested wolf reluctance to cross fladry barriers by using it to block the path between wolves and a yummy deer carcass.

Setting the flagging and bait, and then a motion-detector automatic counter, Lance began an investigation that contrasted wolf wariness with voracity. If the carcass was unprotected, the wolves responded as expected, all packs set upon the feast within about five minutes of it being put in their pen. In contrast, fladry kept the wary wolves at bay for a day. A single day of protection would not be long enough for calves in a pasture, so he upped the game and bolstered the fladry by stringing it on electric fence line. Its scariness was reinforced with a painful jolt, and the wolves were repelled for weeks.

Lance's wolf packs responded similarly to Patrick Darrow's coyotes in that the animals used different strategies for overcoming the virtual threat that stood between them and the food. Even after being zapped, some wolves tested the barrier frequently. Three bold and persistent packs tried over seven hundred times to find a way to cross the barrier. Some made five hundred attempts, some three hundred. Others made only fifty attempts. Then finally the shy ones: zero.[6] Packs of wolves separated themselves into different cultures of predatory aggressiveness or prey-like shyness or persistent optimizers, just like Darrow's lowly coyotes.

Patrick Darrow's coyotes and Nate Lance's wolves, both groups of wild predators well-suited to their environments, provide two examples of how the carnivorous beast must balance the needs of their gut while protecting their hides. Not just an academic amusement, the interplay between filling a stomach and saving a skin has particular relevance as applied research. When creating devices that frighten predators in order to protect human resources, the variation in animals has been a source of frustration for scientists. It is also, however, a source of knowledge, a demonstration of how important understanding animal personality is for wildlife management.

More recent graduate students, such as Patrick Myers, are lucky to be observing animals now.[7] It's different for students these days as they don't have the same fundamentalist baggage to rebel against that old scientists such as myself have. Indeed, my conversation with Myers revealed that he based his understanding on a few now-accepted themes, such as, "We all know our pets have personality, because we spend the time with them. If we spent as much time with wild animals, we'd see the same thing." Another was, "I don't think it is anthropomorphizing to acknowledge that every animal is unique." Times have changed since I was in graduate school.

Myers, currently a graduate student, had worked for the United States Park Service where he specialized in recovery of species such as Channel Island fox and California condors. He worked with animals in captive and wild situations, where he was able to observe individuals closely. For example, he helped to pair young California condors with "mentor" birds: adults that could demonstrate to inexperienced birds important condor techniques, such as how to pry into carcasses. Myers observed that each condor was different. Some were reluctant, some bold, some shy. He could tell them apart by their behaviors, and although condors are not the most loveable as fetid-meat-consuming scavengers, he had favorites.

The Channel Island foxes varied too. Myers told me about how drastically differently the various animals would react in similar situations. When trapping, some would be full of "piss and vinegar and be trying to bite your hand off." Others, blindfolded, would literally curl up in his lap and sleep as he examined them. The young researcher's early work experiences primed him for studying individual variation in animals. Now a graduate student at Utah State University, Myers was hired to examine the success of rehabilitating black bears and releasing them back into the wild. It could be risky to release them, because black bears, like the other predators we have discussed, sometimes kill people.

A few hours' drive from Myers's home in Logan, Utah, an eleven-year-old boy was pulled from his tent by a black bear in 2011.[8] On August 15, 2013, a twelve-year-old girl was attacked by a bear near her home in Cadillac, Michigan. A rash of six attacks was reported across the country that week.[9] Black bears can be formidable, and the biggest of eastern North America may achieve eight hundred pounds in weight, but three hundred pounds is more likely for a male and two hundred for a female. Small bears are powerful enough to smack down the biggest human wrestler, but even a mother black bear with cubs is more likely to order her young up a tree and run rather than attack a human unfortunate enough to come between them. Stephen Herrero documented five hundred bear attacks in his book *Bear Attacks: Their Causes and Avoidance*.[10] For such a powerful animal, it is surprising that 90 percent of injuries they cause don't even begin to approach lethality. Black bears range across the United States, but the frequency of attacks is low; from 1900 to 1980, twenty-three human fatalities were recorded. There are many more opportunities for black bears to attack than the bruins take advantage of. Only a rare few have aggresive personalities.

Thinking of the observed variation in black bear behavior, Myers observes, "If humans are animals and have personalities, it's a minor logical walk to the notion that because other animals are animals like humans, they'd have similar feelings of pain or emotion. It is a greater leap to argue that the other animals don't have individuality or emotions." We do ourselves a disservice in our role as animals if we deny the similarities between humans and other animals like bears.

The reason we separate ourselves from the other animals, Myers supposes, results from cognitive dissonance. He is as much a philosopher as a biologist and does not neglect the more profound ramifications of his research and worldview. He goes on to assert that we part ourselves from other animals because it eliminates our accountability for our actions. He smiles sardonically at his cynical musings, but he assures me that it is easier to choose and justify our own self-interest if we can trivialize the existence of other species. Sometimes it is the result of human hubris, but other people are "willingly ignorant," he says. The point of Myers's research is to provide knowledge, because "the more information that people have, the more ability they have to get past societal blinders and to respect animals."[11]

Myers infers that if we know more about other people or animals, it will change how we view and treat them. I jump to the moral implications and ask, "Do you have a different moral obligation to a deer you know versus one you don't?" His response is that it depends on the individual human. Because we are all different, many of us will come to different conclusions, even given the same information. Because of individuality, even objectivity is subjective.

I remember why I so much enjoy working with graduate students.

Myers's optimistic research ironically resulted from unfortunate events: a hunter, breaking the regulations and killing a female bear, may have orphaned her offspring; or more often, it was an accident on the road where a mother bear was killed and her cubs were left bawling on the side of the road. In such situations, Utah's policy was to rehabilitate the cubs. They would be moved to a facility where the baby bears could be bottle-fed if they were very young, and then transitioned to natural foods as soon as possible. This was the pool from which Myers drew his subjects. Specifically, he was examining how different individual orphaned bears are. He was trying to match the personality of the orphans with how successful they would be at prospering after release back into the wild.

Myers made an obvious effort to be objective, using numbers for the animals that he studied: F1401, F1402, M1403, M1404, M1405, M1406. He was forced to be more descriptive, however, because the staff who helped care for his bears rebelled: they would not accept only numbers as identifiers. Pressured to name the bears, Myers sheepishly came up with the names Ruby, D, Cisco, Sonny, Leadbelly, and Joe Hill. Joe Hill was a prominent Utah labor rights activist. Cisco, Sonny, and Leadbelly were plucked from Bob Dylan's "Song to Woody."

To describe bear temperament, Myers didn't want to automatically accept preconceived behavioral categories, such as the five-factor approach. He wanted to think like a bear and to tailor observations to the animals that were being observed. So he first sat and watched a focal animal, gathering information to come up with

categories relevant to the bears in the context of captivity, rehabilitation, and release. He devised trials where he tested the bears for their
response to a novel object, startled them with an unfamiliar sound,
and watched how they approached something new. A shy or nervous
bear would not readily approach a novel object but would examine it
from a distance by sliding along the pen walls. Myers observed how
bears would jump and startle when he played the sound of two rac-
coons fighting. "They had all had rides in trailers and were familiar
with anthropogenic noise sources," such as horns and engines and
everything in the human world. The snarling of two little critters
was the best novel neutral sound he could find.

In Myers's research, different bears responded differently, of
course, but Joe Hill stood out. Joe had ended up in the rehabilitation
pen by getting into trouble foraging in the town of Moab, Utah. Joe
was obviously different from the other bears right from the start.
Most notable was that he had a different sleep schedule. The other,
"normal" bears were most active in the morning and evening. Joe
tended to sleep when the other bears were most active. He wasn't
afraid of new things either. He'd approach readily when the other
bears were cautious. Joe Hill did not stick to the edges of the pen
but went boldly right into the middle. "The other bears were more
subtle," Myers said.

Based on his observations of the bears and other species, Myers
formed his own theory of how personalities develop. Younger animals, Myers theorized, will be more successful to rehabilitate, because they are still early in their development, but older animals are
stuck in their ways. He used a mountain metaphor to explain.

A large peak will come to a pinnacle, building upon ascending
and converging ridges that further subdivide toward the base of the
mountain. Myers's metaphor is that behavior develops within individuals like a drop of water placed at the tip of the peak. Inputs may
always be small, like wind blowing the drop to the east or the west,
but at the top of the mountain a small nudge will lead to a drastically
different outcome. A tiny nudge early in the trip dictates whether a
drop ends up on the north or south side of the mountain, an early
difference of an inch results in a later difference of miles. If the drop
is most of the way down, however, it can be blown equivalent inches

in any direction, but the movement will have a much smaller effect when the drop reaches the base. That's how he explains behavioral development. We are all rushing to the same valley floor along a baseline that is our personality, but early experiences have a greater impact on how we act when we are older. For Myers's bears, the metaphorical distances have real significance. If the wrong behavioral path is taken early, there is much more distance to correct later. As a result, some problem bears may not be fixable.

As apex predators such as bears and wolves eat their way down into the food web, each strand plucks against others throughout the ecosystem. This top-to-bottom disruption of species abundance and composition is termed a *trophic cascade* by ecologists and has become a popular narrative for science writers.[12] Trophic cascades result in the alteration of landscapes due to changes in herbivore impacts on the range.[13] What's more, differences in deer or elk behavior—as they balance their quest to forage with their avoidance of predators—can lead to revitalized ecosystems.

Shortly after the turn of the century, Bill Ripple at Oregon State University boldly announced the most famous trophic cascade; he asserted that the presence of wolves in Yellowstone National Park corresponded with dramatic change in the vegetative landscape.[14] Wolves have been absent from Yellowstone since the early part of the twentieth century, and elk populations flourished during that time. Elk, not threatened by predators, took advantage of foraging in places that would have been dicey choices had predators inhabited an intact ecosystem. Without wolves as a threat, elk ranged into the meadows with impunity and the vegetation (their "prey") suffered. Aspen and cottonwood sprouts were being grazed to death and Yellowstone's northern range was struggling against the onslaught.

After wolves returned and their populations grew, the predators quickly culled bold elk. It is argued that aspen now grow better and higher in riparian areas encircled by wolf territories because fearless elk, which wander out of cover in wolf country, die. Wary elk live, but they do it by avoiding the open areas and sparing young aspen. Fear is the engine of wariness and thus survival for all prey species.[15]

Just as predator species as a whole balance wariness with aggression, prey species exhibit personality types both fearful and outgoing, and their *individual behaviors* create ecological impacts bigger than the species themselves.

———

Before the 1990s, an elk in Banff, Alberta, was a rare sight, but now, a new type of "townie" elk has adapted to invading the suburbs.[16] Aggressive elk have recently been known to intimidate humans, causing road hazards and a general nuisance in Alberta.

A graduate student with the University of Alberta, Robert Found, created a PhD project out of approaching elk and strewing salvaged bits of bicycle in their foraging fields. Using cameras to monitor the novel objects, he measured how different elk approached the items that he introduced. As an interesting side note, he also tested *lateralization*, or handedness, in his elk. Yes, like researchers have done with kangaroos and chimps and a myriad of others, Found determined whether individual elk favored leading with one leg over another through deep winter snows.[17]

As expected, there were bold and shy elk, those that approached novel objects or allowed him to approach closer. Then there were the wary and timid, those afraid of novel objects and potential predators. By continuing the frightening and harassment, Found determined that wariness could be effectively increased in bold elk. The downside, however, was that bold elk went back to their old, bold ways quickly. They could learn, but they were inherently bold, and when the frightening stimuli were taken away, those elk quickly forgot about it.

It seems extraneous, but he also found a link between handedness and other aspects of an elk's personality. Some elk were ambidextrous and didn't favor a leg. Others had definite handedness. Laterality in an elk said something about that elk's sense of purpose, its strength of personality. As some people are wavering and variable in decisions and others have a singular and precise view and desire for the world, the elk that favored a leg were set in their ways; they always responded in a similar manner, maintaining the same predictable threshold of tolerance for a threat. Elk without lateralization, however, were more variable. As if they could not choose whether to run or stay or which leg to lead with, they were less predictable in their responses. Laterality is difficult to define in this context, and it is not a description of a personality type such as bold or shy, but it means something akin to a dependable personality, like someone who is even-keeled and consistent versus a flighty or capricious companion.

———

Lynne Gilbert-Norton, animal behavior consultant with Pets Decoded in Salt Lake City, knows that dogs vary and that certain personality types tend to cause the most difficulties.[18] Individual dogs fall differently on the predator to prey personality continuum, but, ironically, Gilbert-Norton worries less about the confident dogs, who act self-assuredly, like they are at the top of the food chain. She says, "Eighty percent of problems I see are with nervous, shy dogs," the ones who succumb to their fear of becoming something else's snack. How do they get that way?

Some nervous individuals lack socialization when young; when at the top of their behavioral mountain journey, the pups don't learn how to navigate the strange ways of humans. Also, dogs have a few susceptible periods during their emotional development. Something can occur that scares a twelve-month-old dog that can cause fear the rest of its life. Or, fearful behavior could be just something inherent in the dog. "Some dogs can be raised in the worst situations and turn out fine," Gilbert-Norton says, but the opposite can also occur. A loving couple can raise a dog under the most caring and considerate of circumstances, and their pet can still develop an intense fear of the world.

It is certainly useful to understand what makes a dog tick, especially one that's a close companion with some difficult quirks. To a behavioral consultant such as Gilbert-Norton, however, the nature versus nurture argument is largely irrelevant. It's what we do with the animal the way it is now that is important. It becomes essential to place a fearful, shy dog with the right person, someone who speaks the dog's language a little. Interspecies communication, Gilbert-Norton asserts, is the key. Both human and dog must listen and learn from each other. If the owner doesn't acknowledge where the dog is coming from and try to determine what its motivations are—from a dog's perspective—the relationship can be disastrous.

It's not a hard and fast rule, but many of the visually oriented breeds tend to favor their predatory instincts. Certain breeds tend to be scrappy—for instance, a little terrier who is absolutely fearless, who chases, barks, and snarls at every bike rider that goes by. How can such a little snack be so ironically ferocious? Then there are the fearful dogs Gilbert-Norton spends more time with. Laurel Braitman, the author of *Animal Wise*, described her beloved Oliver in a poignant example. Oliver—a powerful Bernese mountain dog was so nervous when left alone that he jumped out of a fourth story window. His mind did not fit the sturdiness of his body, and he was overcome, mad with fear.[19]

Dogs are familiar to us. They provide abundant anecdotes of contrast: some are powerful beasts afraid of their own shadow, while there are puny pugs whose bravery far outpaces their physique. The science, however, isn't just about how the personalities manifest under the wings of human guardians, but about how creatures of the field balance opportunities and dangers in natural systems. Seemingly counterproductive personalities do not appear to make sense, at first look, relative to natural selection. So researchers are probing how the predator-prey continuum balances within populations over generations. To do that, they turned to species known for predatory rapacity and short generations rather than canine cuddliness

———

One reason the study of animal personality hasn't had the mainstream splash it deserves is because many of the study subjects are less glamorous species. Mammalian predators, such as wolves and bears and dogs, are exciting and charismatic and often the subject of scientific research and popular accounts. But due to their relatively long life spans and small population, expanded studies of their predatory nature in the context of evolution and natural selection are limited. If researchers want to ask the big questions, sometimes we need small subjects. Thus, we return to the most voracious species, spiders, to examine the interplay between predator and prey and how the continuum develops in individuals.

Fishing spiders (*Dolomedes triton*) stalk around the edges of cattail ponds and ambush prey (such as earwigs and wolf spiders) like eight-legged mountain lions. Except mountain lions have the benefit of not simultaneously having birds, bats, and fish stalking them, as fishing spiders do. Fishing spiders have a superpower, however, and when their spider sense detects airborne and waterborne vibrations, they dive into the water and cling to aquatic vegetation or the underside of rocks. They create little space suits of air bubbles around them so that when they are ready to emerge, they can come to the surface completely dry—even after being submerged for thirty to ninety minutes.

Chadwick Johnson and Andrew Sih, bold leaders in the study of animal personality, collected sixty of the little spiders and raised them in plastic tubs.[20] The floors of the tubs were covered with water within which floated a chunk of Styrofoam to give the spiders places to dive and hide. The researchers followed the spiders as they grew up, from juvenile through adulthood, for about six months. That may seem brief, but so much happens so fast in spider lives. The researchers measured the boldness of each spider, both in its resistance to running away and in its tendency to dive and stay submerged in response to a potential threat. The scientists simulated a potential threat by sneaking up behind a spider and poking it in the butt with a pencil. This is why I love science: discovering the amazing using the commonplace.

The problem for a hiding spider is that although it is not susceptible to being preyed upon when under water, it is also unable to forage. So, evolutionarily, timidity has its advantages (a hiding spider is a spider that doesn't get eaten) and its drawbacks (a hiding spider is a starving spider). How does an animal "choose" to balance satisfying its own desires against detrimentally satisfying the desires of another animal? To measure personality type on that continuum, Johnson and Sih dropped a cricket into the water above a startled and submerged spider. Submerged spiders are known to be able to detect potential prey when they are under water; so, the researchers could measure how brave the different spiders were by measuring how long it took each spider to return to the surface to attack the prey. The researchers cleverly evaluated the continuity of personality through time too, by testing the spiders as juveniles and through adulthood.

Johnson and Sih also considered the other primal, carnal appetite. The best reason to eat, at least evolutionarily, is to survive long enough to have sex. So the researchers not only dangled food above the tub of submerged spiders but they also introduced strapping males above the submerged females. Male fishing spiders detect nearby adult females from the perfume of pheromones that she leaves about. If he can tell that a female is nearby, he will tap the water surface creating ripples with his front legs in order to woo her. How brave the female was in the context of mating was determined by measuring how long she took to emerge to court. The significance of spider behavior in Johnson and Sih's world boiled down to the soap operas that played out within the tubs, because staying safe enough to mate is useful only if one is not *too* safe to find a mate.

The researchers found that spiders differed, and that each spider's response was shaped by the context in which they were tested: whether or not there was food or a potential mate nearby. Females that were less concerned about leaving safety for food were also braver in trading safety for a mate. Overall, the females were less wary around potential foods than potential mates, like tweens at a school dance, but the researchers did not investigate that effect. Still, similar to bluebirds and troubled Bernese mountain dogs, the female's confidence wasn't the result of physical size but of innate bravery. Fishing spiders—a species that lives for only six months— exhibit individual personalities that are consistent over time, just like the "more advanced" species we've examined. A spider who was bold when young, who refused to run and hide, or who would hide only for a short period after being prodded tended also to be bold when older. Researchers are finding demonstrable personalities—animals that balance all life's appetites—wherever they look.

Even lowly fiddler crabs (*Uca mjoebergi*) side-walk their way with individual distinctiveness on Australian beaches. The male crabs are easily distinguished from females because of the huge front claws, which they use for love and war: courtship with females and fights with other males. The crabs are also rather easy to track and observe individually, because they keep to their own burrows, holes in the sand that are essential for survival. Without the cover and protection of their sand holes, the little crabs would die as snacks for avian predators or desiccate in the dry, hot sun.

Although it hasn't been that way for me, wildlife biology actually can be as glamorous as nature shows portray: Leeann Reaney and Patricia Backwell found a way to pursue cutting-edge science while sitting on the beach. Specifically, the researchers observed fiddler crabs on the shoreline to determine how crabs varied in their individual responses as ruthless predator or timid prey item.[21]

To scare the crabs, Reaney and Backwell strung a line and a pulley over the surface of the sand and flew an artificial bird across the sandy flats. Sensing the shadow of an avian attack, the frightened little crabs would dash to their burrows for protection. All would not emerge from their caves at the same time, however. Brave ones were frightened only for a moment and returned to the surface in fewer than twenty-five seconds. Others, chickens of the sea, remained hiding for more than four and a half minutes.

As with other species that scientists have examined, the investigators identified bold and shy crabs: some were more aggressive while others were ruled more by fear of becoming prey themselves. This was a behavioral trait and not a physiological one too, as there wasn't a correlation between boldness and size. Furthermore, individuality was consistent over time; in repeated trials, quick emergers continued to be quick emergers, and slow ones consistently always stayed in their burrows longer. Bold males were more aggressive among each other too, fighting more among themselves. Such bullies were also more likely to kick another animal out and steal its burrow. In contrast, when the bullied crabs were displaced, they would find an unoccupied burrow rather than start a fight to conquer another.

How does aggressiveness and claw size correlate with reproductive success? For females of the species, courtship is essentially window shopping. When ready to mate, females leave their burrows and move among the throngs of males on the sand. The males vigorously wave their large claw to try to entice the females into their love nests. After the female chooses, the lucky male seals the two in his burrow where they remain until she lays her eggs.

What exactly does a female crab look for in a mate? To study that aspect of crab culture, the researchers used video recordings to measure each male's prowess with his claw by counting how fast he waved while beckoning females.

The results were intriguing, and another example of the importance of measuring behavior and personality—but keeping the two separated. The researchers had already determined the predator versus prey personality type of the male crabs. If they hadn't, they would have missed the essential component of crab mating rituals. Examining the crabs as they would have in the past, looking at obvious morphological and behavioral characteristics such as the size of a male's claw or how fast he waved it, it would have been difficult for researchers to determine why females chose which males to mate with. The brave and timid male crabs waved their claws at equivalent rates. They had various claw sizes. Reaney and Backwell concluded that the females were not paying attention to claw size nor to the way the males waved them. All the different males had equal access to the females too, but the researchers found a strong difference in female choice toward suitors. Specifically, the females offered to mate with a brave male 89 percent of the time. It wasn't physiology, dance moves, or the size of their appendage that the females were looking for. It was a male's personality that seduced them. Too often we expect the obvious, the things we can easily see and measure, such as an animal's size or a particular behavior, but in the context of the threat of predation, the difficult thing to measure, personality, can be more important in the long run.

———

As broad a survey as I am making in this book, it is important to admit that I am only beginning to touch on the whole of the fascinating subject of animal personality. Elsewhere there are more thorough academic descriptions of the primary research that has moved the science from anathema to mainstream study,[22] and within them all is one species that is the exemplar of the subject: the great tit, *Parus major*.

A little Old World bird, the great tit looks a lot like an olive-breasted version of the black-capped chickadee in North America. It may be mostly unknown to North Americans, but the personality literature on great tits is much larger than the diminutive species itself.

Great tits are a common and easy species to work with, and they don't require far-flung travels for European professors. John Quinn, for example, when with the ornithology group at the University of Oxford, had to jaunt no farther than four miles from campus to find birds in Wytham Wood.[23] Common little birds, yes, but priceless for understanding how important personality is within species.

Quinn and his fellow researchers were curious about how great tits trade off the risk of starvation by not foraging with the risk of sudden death by becoming prey themselves. Great tits eat nuts and berries in the fall and winter, but they are predators in the spring and summer, when they hunt a wide variety of insects. The researchers created patches of good and minimal food in the forests and placed the feeding stations both near cover and in the open in order to create the mix of conditions, from good food and high predation risk to poor food and low predation risk. The good food stations had whole nuts, whereas the poor foods had smaller and less attractive granules. The open feeders left the tits vulnerable to attack by their nemesis, the sparrow hawk (*Accipiter nisus*). The threat to a great tit exposed in the open is significant due to sparrow hawks' prowess as predators. The raptor is a master of death-from-above ambush, flying in to attack at speeds of up to fifty-five miles per hour.

Quinn and colleagues were quite clever in how they measured which bird went to which foraging place, and how the birds balanced the risk of predation with the reward of good food. When they captured the tits for behavioral assays, researchers fitted the little birds with passive integrated transponders (PIT) tags. Like little rice grains, PIT tags are the same devices that veterinarians inject under a dog's scruff so that they can be identified with a special electronic reader. By placing a PIT reader and data logger under each feeding station, the researchers used an automated system to count which bird went where.

To assay a bird's braveness or, more specifically, how readily it searched through a novel environment, the researchers released each bird into a room and recorded its number of hops and flights as it explored new perches and investigated the new surroundings. In their study, a brave bird would be one who was active and fast in learning about the new surroundings. A timid animal was one who was more reluctant to expose itself while traipsing through an unfamiliar environment.

Overall, the results were clear and consistent. As a group, the birds used the good feeder less when it was put into an exposed and dangerous position, especially during the afternoon when sparrow hawks were on the prowl. As a group, the birds traded their need to forage efficiently with the need to minimize risk of predation. Males and females and birds of different ages—the way animals are normally categorized—showed little difference in how they balanced eating with predation risk.

Accounting for individuals, however, the researchers found differences between them in their bravery scores. Another example of the breadth of species that are easily observed to exhibit personality types, brave great tits tended to prioritize feeding on the high quality food first thing in the morning and during the day. Timid great tits were more afraid of being prey themselves than going hungry.

Spiders, birds—how widespread is an animal's tendency to balance their appetites with becoming an appetizer?

⎯⎯⎯

Andrew Sih, whom I refer to frequently in this book, is a great father of the field of animal personality. His work has added not only great depth but also great breadth to the discipline as he's studied species from spiders to other seemingly simple organisms such as sunfish (*Lepomis cyanellus*). I had never before given fish much credit for being able to feel, much less to behave or show personality, but Sih has spent much of his career focusing on fish behaviors and those of the little larval salamanders (*Ambystoma barbouri*) that they eat.[24]

Sih's conclusion about the challenge of life was straightforward and simple: "Above all, don't get eaten." His reasoning suggested a preference toward being a timid creature, avoiding the dangers of life. But intriguingly, Sih's own work showed even that maxim is not absolute.

Sih, throwing off the shackles of behaviorist dogma, noticed early on in his research life that some salamanders made certain peculiar choices, ones that didn't seem to make sense. Some salamanders explored new areas of their tanks while their homebody brethren remained in dark and safe locations. There were clearly different types of larval salamanders.[25]

To investigate more thoroughly, Sih and his colleagues observed streamside salamander larvae and their interactions with their nemesis, green sunfish.[26] The two species are common in small streams in the southeastern United States, and they live in streams that aren't narrow continuous channels, but rather are a series of pools and riffles bestrewing a waterway. The sunfish are generalist predators, meaning that they will snack on bugs, tadpoles, and smaller fish. Salamanders, which primarily exist in pools, are prey to the fish, but they are also predators themselves, dining on benthic insects and zooplankton. A subtle clue, foreshadowing the story, is that streams are composed of a series of pools, some pools with fish and some without.

Sih, then working at the University of Kentucky, traveled fifteen miles from Lexington to Raven Run Creek to capture larvae. To evaluate individual responses of the larval salamanders, he and his colleagues needed to observe their subjects' responses to the presence of predators, but they had to do it in a way that was safe for the little larval salamanders. To do this, they first created sunfish perfume by holding the predators in an isolated tank for a while and then used the fish water as eau de sunfish with which to test the bravery of salamanders. They acknowledged in their paper, "We used fish chemical cues rather than free-swimming fish to ensure that we would get sufficient data on each individual (i.e., if we had exposed larvae to free-swimming fish, many larvae would have been consumed before we had much information on their behaviour)."[27] Scientists can be funny too.

In earlier work, Sih determined that it made sense to stay safe in the shadows, especially when predatory sunfish were swimming about in the water column. That some of his subjects darted into danger was a perplexing observation for him. In the wild, a salamander that went out into the exposed water column was almost always eaten, which broke the base rule of his understanding (don't get eaten). It was contrary to the idea of natural selection. How could such a trait that so clearly meant you were going to die before reproducing still exist in the species?

Many aspects of Sih's work are notable, but in this particular experiment he and his colleagues concluded that certain individuals and their kin moved out into the exposed areas of experimental tanks consistently, whether or not dangerous sunfish cues were present. These salamanders had predatory personality types, and they were focused on finding food. Other salamanders and their kin stayed in the safer places whether or not sunfish cues were apparent; they were more worried about becoming prey.

The key to understanding why there are brave salamanders in the population even though they are almost always eaten is in understanding the variability of the rivers and pools where the salamanders live. Fish don't bespeckle streams uniformly, and a larval salamander can find itself in a pool with a plethora of fish or in a pool devoid of them. Little baby salamanders, by choosing different life paths, are essentially taking bets. If a salamander larvae swims into the open and a lot of fish are around, it will be eaten. But the sunny openness also produces more food. In that environment—without fish—a brave salamander will gorge on the abundance, be fed well, and will grow faster. Indeed, Sih and others have found that such salamanders, due to their behavioral choices, grow bigger and more rapidly. Even better, Sih explains, their wanderings tend to expose them to the currents at night, which allows them to escape from pools safely, while their shy colleagues remain trapped by their listlessness. Finally, although brave hunters may be more likely to become prey themselves, they have another benefit by growing faster. If the pool they are in dries up before they are grown, as can happen to the timid ones, only the well-fed salamanders will survive.

Because environments differ, some individuals benefit in some circumstances and others gain in different ecological conditions. If you are a brave salamander in a fishless pool, you are going to outcompete your wary brethren. If you are a brave salamander in a pool chock full of fish, you will lose the natural-selection dice roll. Relative to evolution, the binding glue that explains the rest of biology, variability in animals is not a nuisance parameter that makes the scientific task of modeling ecological systems difficult. Rather, individual variation is the fundamental driver of the success of life on the earth. Without differences between individuals, there would be no evolution.

CHAPTER 5

Herd or Hermit

A portmanteau of *equine* and *synergy*, Elizabeth Liverman's Equisyn uses horses to help people better connect with their emotions.[1] "It is an approach similar to life coaching, combined with equine-assisted psychotherapy." As we sit at a picnic table next to a riding ring at her Goochland, Virginia, farm, she talks of chakras and deep power work, but I am most interested in how she uses horses to center people emotionally. More specifically, how she matches a particular person to a particular horse.

"We tend to help people with deep emotional or mental processing," Elizabeth says, "the types of scars left in victims of child sexual abuse." Most of her clients are dealing with topics and emotions that are "very, very difficult to work with," and Equisyn assists with many types of trauma. A client may be addressing anything from the trauma of a career change to finally dealing with an early event festering within.

Liverman is a certified Equine Gestalt practitioner and has great faith in her horses. She sees horses as especially effective tools, and sometimes even teachers. The most notable difference between most people and horses is that "horses live in the moment." People get caught up in things, extrinsic factors. They overthink or focus on something other than the here and now. Listening to Liverman describe the day-to-day attitude of a resting pony, I think the Dalai Lama has not achieved more enlightenment than a horse in a pasture.

Pursuing work with horses was a natural progression for Liverman. Over the years working in stables, riding for shows, and playing with them every chance she could get, she has interacted with hundreds of horses. "I've ridden a ton, but there may be only thirty-five or forty that I really knew in a deeper, closer, way." She began riding when she was twelve, a prime age for girls in love with horses, but her obsession started when she was much younger. She recalls running through house hallways on all fours and whinnying. When criticized by her older sister, Elizabeth responded, "Mom told me that I can be anything I want when I grow up. I'm going to be a horse."

Liverman uses Melissa Pierce's "Touched by a Horse" techniques to engage troubled souls.[2] Liverman cautions that the process is not simply a matter of putting any person with any horse in the middle of a corral. It is a matter of finding two beings with matching or complementary personalities. When the human-horse pair is right, the horse nudges at the right time. It walks away at the right time or comforts on cue. The right horse will bring out feelings of trust in the most guarded person. The horses create a mode of communication and bonding that allows clients to peer more honestly into themselves.

Liverman explains that horse communication is subtle, which slows people down and steers them to a state of introspection. She asserts that she has not trained her horses. Moreover, she insists that she *couldn't* train the horses to do the work. If the horse does not like a person—and it happens—the technique won't work with that client. Besides, she points out, the therapy is not about the horse. The important aspect is not trying to train an unwilling horse to work, but rather teaching people to listen. The first step is pairing the right horse with the client, which I imagined to be difficult. We can't read horses' minds, and they don't speak. They are subtle, as Liverman says. She corrects me and insists that pairing person and horse is easy. She just lets the horses choose for themselves.

I ask her about the differences in her horses and how they choose a human, and she responds as if she'd done a PhD on the topic, precisely defining each horse in her stable.

"Gian is ESTP," she says, using the Myers-Biggs abbreviation. Having so much difficulty in trying to define personality in animals myself, I was both surprised and a bit jealous of the degree of detail with which she could describe her horses. Gian, a big Hanoverian cross—known in horse circles as a warmblood—falls into the personality categories of extravert, sensing, thinking, perceiving. He focuses on the outside world, interprets it, thinks it through, and stays open and free with options. "He has no work ethic," Liverman chuckles. He's outgoing, but does not want to go do a job just to do a job. "He wants to know why to do the job."

Starlight is a black Tennessee walker who is "amazing with people. INFJ." He's sort of the opposite of Gian. Introverted. Intuitive. Feeling. Judging. "He is intuitive, sensitive to people's energy. He works really well with people that are NF. He has more difficulty working with people that are ST." Sensing, thinking, like Gian. It's that ST people just aren't as in the moment as horses are. "If a person is not present, Starlight will not interact with them." The person has to listen.

She recounts a story about a group of clients that had come in for a session. Liverman always does a safety demonstration first—"They are horses, after all"—and pretty big compared to you and me. She put the clients into the working pen with Starlight and let the horse and people try to figure out their relationships. She does not interact with clients and horses during such introductions, but simply watches from outside the pen. On that occasion, Starlight ignored all but one client, whom she stared at, focusing completely on her.

"I get the feeling that this horse wants to work with *me*," said the client. With that, Starlight moved toward her and nuzzled her chest, then around her abdomen, and then throat. The woman burst into tears.

"You hear about dogs that sniff out when people are going to have a seizure or can detect diabetes or something." Liverman translates the significance of the interaction. The woman had a malignant tumor in her abdomen. The client was traumatized, and the horse picked her out of the lineup and nudged the source of concern. The connections between human and beast are amazing, and we humans understand only a small portion of them.

Liverman and Starlight continued working with the client. Opening to her emotions, she summed up her troubles as "my heart really hurts, and I feel that I can't express myself and what is happening."

Liverman instructed the emotionally fragile woman to walk around the pen, and Starlight, on his own accord, followed her, his nose inches away from her back. "What does it feel like when you want to communicate but can't?" she asked the client.

The woman stopped, but Starlight continued on and moved in front of her, blocking her path. He dropped his ears and rubbed his head against her chest, his forehead catching her gentle tears. She wrapped her arms around him. After a few moments, the client looked up and Starlight backed away.

The emotional work that Liverman does is slow and indirect. She doesn't analyze, and in that particular situation she simply instructed the client to continue walking around the pen. Starlight moved behind and followed, but this time he held his muzzle against the client, keeping contact with her shoulder blades.

"Do you feel like you can talk about it better now?" Liverman inquired.

The client, feeling better, responded with a yes.

"Why?"

"He's got my back," she said.

"I know it sounds woo-woo," Liverman admits, but at its base it doesn't have to be magical or spiritual. It only requires being present in the moment and to "listen to horses. They communicate, but they do it in a very intuitive way."

It is impossible to quell Liverman's enthusiasm for her horses. She can't help but describe each to others such as myself, sipping a cold drink in a spot of shade along her riding ring. There is Cody, the mustang-paint cross. She laughs when she talks about him, describing him as *definitely* ENFP: extrovert, intuitive, feeling, perceiving. "He's outgoing, loves everyone. He loves to play. He is the one horse who gets into the pen who will make everyone laugh." Cody is also particularly good with kids. "You can put a baby on his back and he'll be the most careful horse in the world."

Fairen is a Thoroughbred who was never raced, and Liverman categorizes him as ISTJ: introvert, sensing, thinking, judging. "He's not outgoing at all. He wants to get the job done and then wants to get out of the pen." Cookie, the mini, she labels INFP. "She's more shy and introverted than the others, but she has no problem letting me lead her around and pet her." The little horse stands about as high as an adult human's hips. "She'll do what you want, but wants it to be fun." It may have something to do with size, but it is definitely an aspect of minihorse personality that Cookie likes kids more than adults.

The final horse we visited was Hank. He had an odd stance about him that even I, much less familiar with horses than Liverman, could readily see. His butt was a square block, not a rounded rump like most horses have. "Hank was a rescue, he's thin still, for certain, but you should have seen him when I got him," she says. "It was terrible." I wonder, after seeing the connection that people can have with individual horses, what kind of interaction would lead to starving one's own horse. Liverman pegs him as ISFJ. Maybe one ought to expect him to be pensive after what he had been through, and she asserts that Hank "likes to think about things. He wants to know what is needed, and then he'll do it." Perhaps he feels security in knowing what is coming next and what his herd mates want of him.

———

When we think of social animals, those living in herds and communities, we think of species such as horses, wolves, or humans. Then, we think about the opposites, solitary animals that tolerate each other only infrequently, perhaps once a year to mate, such as bears or wolverines. Perhaps we don't even think about the lives of insects and arachnids, but we ought to. Worlds of behavior and cooperation occur in species far different from *Homo sapiens*, and if we are going to give animals credit, it shouldn't be due only to their charisma and humanlike emotional proclivities.

Think again about spiders. The voracious little eight-eyed web builders may seem like a strange assemblage of animals within which to go looking for personality, but they not only have individual personalities, as we've seen in previous chapters, they also create complex cultures.

Susan Riechert and Thomas Jones were a pair of the early explorers traipsing around the Everglades in the mid-2000s and investigating the mystery of variability in spider sociality. Road tripping, they journeyed from the southern tip of Florida up through Alabama and into Tennessee and collected twenty-five nests of the spider *Anelosimus studiosus* from various locations along the north-south transect of the three states. The peregrinating investigators took measurements of length, width, and height of each nest and identified the inhabitants within them for individual study.

One thing was immediately apparent. Spiders from the northern, higher latitudes lived communally. They formed colonies that sometimes contained hundreds of females. Southern spiders of the same species, however, lived solely, in solitary webs away from others. The north to south effect was strong, with 71 percent of the variation in colony size being explained by how far north the spiders lived.[3] The spiders from the different locations had different cultures.

What caused the observed differences? How did the spiders from each location create a different set of social rules for interacting with each other? Riechert and Jones tested their subjects by putting two spiders at a time in a box and then watching to see if the spiders would huddle in the same corner or separate. Sometimes, there were two spiders from different solitary nests. Other times they placed two females from the same big colony. Last, they mixed two females from different colonies together. To determine if the personality differences were genetically linked, the scientist tested laboratory-reared babies too.

Sure enough, the southern spiders tended to be loners. When put into the same box, they usually retreated to opposite corners. The spiders from the higher latitudes, whether from the same nest or not, were attracted to stay in the same corner together. Riechert and Jones looked more closely at the individual spiders and determined that the choices of individuals were what powered the formation of whole societies, and other important behavioral aspects were at work too.[4] They noticed a relationship between the social to solo continuum and the tendency to travel: individuals that dispersed from communal nests dispersed shorter distances.

Was it actually spider personality, something inheritable, or was the effect, so closely correlated with latitude, just caused by the environment? It is interesting that transplanting a spider from one habitat to another did not change its attitude regarding getting along with others. Riechert and Jones allowed the spiders in their laboratory to mate and raise their young in order to remove any north-south effect of the environment from the progeny. Using the same share-a-corner box test to measure sociality, the researchers found that spiders with northern parents were far more social than the southern ones. The reason for spiders wanting to live next to each other was innate. Natural selection favored social spiders in some geographic locations. Why?

Uta Seibt and Wolfgang Wickler studied communal spiders in the 1980s and had laid the foundations for Riechert and Jones's work and the evolutionary significance of it.[5] In their analyses, they noted that living in larger colonies created a cost to the individual, because females from large colonies were much smaller than solitary spiders. Since the spiders were smaller, the number of egg cocoons per female was also reduced dramatically. Overall, the research indicated that spiders genetically inclined to be social would have fewer babies. Being less fit in terms of natural selection, why would social spiders persist in populations?

One clue is that social individuals cooperate. They form multifemale colonies with shared web maintenance, prey capture, and cooperative care of offspring (known as alloparental care). The answer is that life is a little harder in cooler places, and a female is more likely to die before her young are ready to leave the nest. In a large group, however, the other colony members can help raise the orphans.[6] Living in groups allows social animals to overcome disadvantages that solitary animals can't. Living in groups requires a predilection for sociality. That personality type allows spiders to live farther north than they otherwise would be able to. Personality and behavior—and not just physiology—allow species to expand their range across the planet.

——

Andrew Sih's influence on animal personality research is ubiquitous, ranging from California, where he resides, to collaborations with researchers such as Stephanie Godfrey in Australia.[7] Together they were expanding notions of the social natures of animals, like sleepy lizards (*Tiliqua rugosa*), and examining how complex groups could form in what most people would consider evolutionary backwaters. By taping GPS units to the tails of sixty lizards in South Australia and recording their activity and position every few minutes, Godfrey and her team mapped out and calculated the associations the lizards made. Did every lizard wander equally among the others? It took some clever math and three years of observation, but using baseline data of how fast and far sleepy lizards usually moved, the researchers calculated expected encounter rates between all the local lizards. That is, what were the chances of any two lizards encountering each other as they went about their daily lizard lives? It was akin to examining people's movements at a cocktail party. Is every person a random social butterfly, spending equal time with everyone in the room, or do people and lizards clump into social networks spending more time near some than others? Do they have favorites? Boyfriends, girlfriends, and friend groups?

It would be a dizzying social event if people moved around like BBs in a box, randomly bouncing into acquaintances. So it goes for sleepy lizards too, who associated with only half the number of lizards they'd visit with if guided purely by chance. Males and females definitely hung out together more than males with males and females with females, which was due to pair bonds between individuals. Sleepy lizards are more of a romantic species, lizard boyfriends and girlfriends traveling together for long periods. The data indicated that lizards not only had favorites but they also had those they loathed and outright avoided. Like lizard high school, cliques of males and females formed that remained stable for the duration of the study.

Animal sociality does not have to look exactly like human society, but there are more similarities among animals, even critters like spiders and lizards or fish, and humans than we give them credit for. Who would have thought that lizards have pair bonds and friend groups? But they do. Is it because of our familiarity with species such as chickens and wolves that we are comfortable with the ideas of pecking orders or alpha males? As if that were not interesting enough in itself, think of the ramifications of social cliques in any species. As groups of individuals assert themselves, how will they form stacks of social connections and hierarchies?

Guppies, *Poecilia reticulata*, are social mixers, but they exhibit elements of individual exceptionalism we expect to find in business books on leadership skills. For instance, publishing in 2013, Culum Brown and Eleanor Irving at Macquarie University New South Wales, Australia, identified personality traits in guppies based on traits that I've described already. Using familiar tests, such as a lone guppy put into a new tank—a perfect analog to research where great tits were placed in novel rooms—the researchers found, as expected, that guppies vary in their tendencies to be aggressive or brave or social.[8] The researchers went a step further, however, after they understood the different personality types of individual fish. They played sociality games, grouping the fish into schools of four, the way college professors collect freshmen into pods for group projects.

As if they'd been observing gaggles of freshmen, Brown and Irving discovered something fascinating in guppies. Based on their composition, the different groups of guppies formed their own "group personality." Fish schools may not be that different from human schools, as cliques take on their own measurable traits, some being more brave or aggressive than others. What was most fascinating was that the groups were not an amalgamation, an average of the individual traits within them. Instead, how the group acted was a function of how active and social its most active and social group member was. As there are fishermen and fishers of men, there are leaders of fish. The authors concluded, "Evidence is emerging that leaders may also differ in terms of their personality," and "that leaders may have intrinsic differences in personality compared to followers."

Leaders, followers, and groups; science is beginning to discover how societies form from collectives of individuals in the natural world. As scientists and authors have begun to look for social networks, they are finding dynamic social groups everywhere. Asian elephants (*Elephas maximus*), for example, are not just a stable group with a single matriarch and linear hierarchical relationships emanating beneath her. Rather, elephants form complicated tiered interactions between individuals, among the whole group, and in pairs. Shermin de Silva and colleagues watched 286 adult female elephants over the course of twenty months and tracked when the pachyderms were in pairs, small groups, and grouped together.[9] The researchers found that elephants formed pairs, but all pairs were not equal. The strength of their bonds differed. The researchers identified six patterns of sociality that ranged from being early-in-the-season buddies to twice-a-year acquaintances. They also found that certain groups of elephants (usually from six to twelve other females) were consistent over the long term. Essentially, the wild elephants had different close friends they spent time with at different times of year, but they maintained their friend groups during the nearly two years of observations. The system of varying associations is known as fission-fusion: an overall group is maintained, but individuals group and ungroup with others in an ebbing and flowing fashion.

Herding like aquatic elephants, schools of dolphins off the coast of Scotland could be expected to act like their terrestrial brethren. They do.[10] David Lusseau, at the University of Aberdeen, along with numerous colleagues, used a lot of boat time, photography, and distinctive scars on dolphins to determine which dolphin swam with which others. Providing an example of how the study of animal behavior can be intensely quantitative, Lusseau and colleagues employed a method called the Girvan-Newman algorithm to mathematically describe dolphin community structure. The model measures how much each dolphin prefers to be with another, then groups the animals that spend the most time together. Furthermore, it evaluates all the associations, drawing together individuals into larger groups with high degrees of internal association. Quantitative methods tend to be data hungry, and fortunately the scientists had 809 schools of dolphins between 1990 and 2002 to examine.

In their analysis, the investigators determined that dolphin social networks were like "small worlds,"[11] with Kevin Bacon–like degrees of connection. Dolphins clustered themselves into dynamic social groups, but any two individuals could be connected by about four steps through linking common acquaintances. Thus, the dolphins followed an equivalent fission-fusion pattern seen in elephants. With the dolphins, however, another characteristic that may seem familiar to us humans was evident.

Dolphin social structure off the Scottish coast was best described as a series of short-term relationships through time, spiced with longer term companions whom they remained associated with for seven to eight years. It is akin to humans interacting with familiar people in our daily lives, talking with neighbors or grocery clerks or church members or subway commuters on the same schedule. Dolphins have friends outside their immediate social networks too, but the associations are more fluid, averaging five years long as opposed to the eight years that the closer social groups remain cohesive. They separate themselves into tribes too.

Humans move through life in loosely associated pods, although we may not even be aware of it, and measuring social behavior of dolphins is like peering into a mirror. We may tend to focus on the repeated, frequent, and more intense interactions, such as with co-working officemates or recreational cliques, but the dolphins' social interactions show us that our social groups are wider than just the sum of our closest friends.

Indeed, finding complicated social interactions between individual animals is likely more a matter of where and how to look than whether or not the social networks exist in other species. Even bats live in colonies with measureable social substructures, from a country-like cave population down to dyads and individuals. The research of Gerald Kerth of the Max Planck Institute for Ornithology and his coauthors provides another example.[12] Through the use of PIT-tagged animals and adroitly positioned readers and data loggers, he and his colleagues created an impressive data set of 20,500 individual roosting observations of wild Bechstein's bat (*Myotis bechsteinii*) over five years. The researchers examined the associations between bats in two colonies and indentified fission-fusion dynamics that were similar to those described for elephants and dolphins. Friendships between bats were not based on physical attributes either, as individuals of different age, size, reproductive status, and relatedness maintained long-term social relationships.

In other mirrorlike observations, the colonies had emergent properties and dynamics larger than the social pairings of any one or two bats. The colonies divided themselves into tribes, which formed from social groupings of several family lineages each, and the members tended not to interact with out-group individuals.

Where there is hope for bats there is with humans also. Even highly isolated bat tribes develop individuals who maintain connection and cross-pollination between different groups. While the rank and file go about the business of their particular group or class, a select few jump across the boundaries that separate the tribes. In human social groups, for example, countries tend to develop classes of elderly statesmen who, like Thomas Jefferson or Benjamin Franklin, remain staunchly loyal to their own ideals while visiting with and chatting up the French.

Kerth and colleagues found a class of diplomats in bats too. Bechstein's bats are ten-gram flying mammals who live for twenty years, so they have plenty of time for creating and dissolving roosting colonies. From April to September, their separate groups convene, like little annual summits; their tribes disintegrate during the winter and then reform every spring. A bat joining a group has the benefit of cooperation, as they share information about foraging, help keep each other warm, and keep each other tidy through allogrooming. Their sociality is multinodal, as the colonies could become isolated, but a class of older bats keeps the animals from overly isolating themselves. They move freely between the colonies, keeping a chain of connection throughout the population.

There are theories that the big brains of mammals such as ourselves developed due to the needs of sociality, but Kerth's conclusions challenged this notion. Sociality becomes apparent even in the unlikeliest of animals if we just take the time to look. Indeed, sociality and connectedness is more integral to all species: cooperating is something all species do and sociality is a measure of it. It's another error of omission due to anthropocentric hubris, and humans aren't really that different from spiders, using social networks and support to live in lands where we could not have otherwise survived, or from bats, establishing different countries but creating social mechanisms—diplomats—that prevent complete isolation.

My fellow graduate students used to say that researchers often take on the characteristics of their scientific subjects, and David Stoner fits that paradigm. Long hair, svelte, he moves slowly and deliberately, but he looks able to launch into a rapid flash of action. Just like the cougars he studies.[13]

Stoner has tracked and monitored around two hundred cougars (*Felis concolor*), and has closely worked with about fifty by his estimation. He is pensive when he describes the individuals, somewhat shy about anthropomorphizing, it seems. He always refers to his cats by their numbers, but they inevitably earned nicknames too. He tells me that the nicknames were given by the rough and tumble houndsmen he worked with, and that it would be inappropriate for him to repeat the sobriquets in polite company.

The scientist admits that his "stomach goes queasy" when people give cuddly names to animals that clearly have no concern for humans, but he acknowledges internal conflict too. Uniquely adept at introspection, especially for a PhD scientist, Stoner points out that he and his fellow biologists wouldn't be in the business if it weren't for a passion for animals. That is to say, it would be dishonest to assert that the motivation is not emotional and that, to wildlife biologists, animals are only cold numbers, a means to a scientific end. Our challenge, rather, is to be cognizant of our emotions and not to let them influence the interpretation of data.

Whether called mountain lion, puma, or cougar, *Felis concolor* is a secretive and solitary species. Stoner laments that due to their near invisibility, his understanding of cougars is less than it could have been. "Our interactions are diluted. We see them once and then all the other interactions are indirect." It is the curse of modern-day wildlife biology. Biologists study "beeps, not behavior." That the cats remain hidden in remote high-mountain areas is likely a primary reason they still exist in the contiguous United States. More obvious larger predators, such as wolves, were wiped out in the Lower 48 by the 1940s, but cougars remained in high mountain enclaves. The lovers of wild animals among us have been growing in number since then, and as a result, the current cougar range covers a swath of the western United States from the coast to the middle of Montana and angles southeast into the lower sections of Texas. The species appears to be expanding as far east as Indiana, moving toward a small remnant population in Florida.

Cougars are known for their stealth and asocial tendencies. Stoner smiles as he describes an occasion when two cougars weren't following the species' script. The most reliable technique for capturing cougars is to use hounds. The dogs sniff the ground, following cougar tracks while barking and creating a commotion. Much like a house cat, a cougar may run for a little while, but will usually climb into a tree to wait out the blustery hounds. On one occasion Stoner had two cougars treed not too far apart from each other. "They were making the strangest sounds," he says. Back and forth. They were communicating. "It was the oddest thing. The two were different." They aren't supposed to be social like that.

Occasions like that spur Stoner to muse, "Our measures of observation are too crude." If we could actually watch the animals interact, what would we find? "We are only seeing the tip of an iceberg. The more we look, the more we see."

For his doctorate, Stoner monitored cougars in a very productive environment, the relatively wet Oquirrh Mountains near Salt Lake City, Utah. There were lots of vegetation and prey in the form of mule deer and even elk. Certain types of cougars live there. Contrasting life in the Oquirrhs with the desert environments of southern Utah and Arizona, he postulated that "a cougar from the Oquirrh Mountains probably wouldn't last ten minutes in the Mojave."

But what if a cougar was moved from the Mojave to the Oquirrhs? His first response was that the cat would probably think it had died and gone to heaven. Then he paused, thinking deeper about the question. The prey base is not the whole story. What the Mojave cats have is space. It is a difficult place to live, but they don't have to compete with lots of other cats either. It may not be a set of skills that drives one cougar to live in the mountains and another to live in the desert. If a cougar is particularly solitary, really a loner, he postulated, it will be much happier in the desert. If it can get along with others nearby, then the highly productive mountain habitats could be a good choice for that individual.

Like Patrick Myers, the graduate student who studies the personalities of orphaned bears, Stoner criticizes himself and his fellow scientists, saying, "We, in our quest to be objective, take the default that animals are robotic. We don't even question it with people . . . it is obvious that we have personalities." He goes on to assert, "Not applying the same reasoning to animals is accepting the negative hypothesis. It's unreasonable." We have to accept that even typically asocial species, such as cougars, are not all stamped out of the same mold. Another important point Stoner makes is surprising, since he works with cougars, a species famed for being regulated by old toms, who maintain exclusive territories and often kill each other. Stoner identifies a bias in how researchers approach science. "Ecology focuses on competition. Our daily activities, actually, are more about cooperation." Humans actually spend a lot of individual energy in cooperation. So do cougars, but scientists just aren't paying attention to it.

Stoner relates an example using one female cougar he followed. "It was Number 6," and her home range overlapped that of another female. During his fieldwork, he documented a time when she was sharing a carcass with another cougar. Cougars, as a rule, are not social animals, but the two were feeding simultaneously. He wasn't certain, but he surmised that the second female was Number 6's mother. The mother, killing a deer, shared it with her five-year-old daughter—and her grandkittens: intergenerational support in a solitary species. Human science is replete with errors of omission: absence of evidence is not evidence of absence. Researchers will surely find more great examples of both individuality and cooperation, but we are only now learning where and how to look.

We do unwittingly focus on extraordinary, if rare, events. It is well known that male cougars cannot live together. They tend to kill each other. Scaled to years and animals, however, such deaths are relative rarities. If killing one another was their prime goal, they would continually search and destroy until there would eventually be no males after the last king died. Instead, they spend more time and energy actually keeping themselves from killing each other. Asocial cougars create a social system where satellite males orbit around a dominant tom's territory. The younger males find ways to eke out a living, while relinquishing prime habitat to the dominant tom. "But we focus on the dramatic fights and death," Stoner observes, "not on how they prevent conflict. It's subtle." What could we learn from solitary animals if we rotated the prism through which we are looking? They fight now and again, but they actually spend much more time not fighting.

The idea of being social or asocial can also be stretched to include interactions with other species. Are cougars intolerant of people? Indeed they are, and their secretiveness is likely what saved them from the antipredator rampages of the early 1800s and 1900s. But all individuals are not the same, and some cougars are more tolerant; they find ways to benefit from people. It's potentially a very rewarding behavior, especially because there aren't many environments that humans don't touch anymore. Stoner cited one particular female as an example. Most cougars remained in the high country, but one female successfully raised kittens on roadkill. With the cornucopia of carcasses, she was a great provider. There is more than one way to feed a cat.

———

The long, sharp ridge of Mount Razorback was only a few miles away, but it was hidden by incessant fog. It would show itself in its entirety a few times a year, but due to the mixing of the angry Bering Sea with the northern Pacific at Adak Island's shores, the island was a treeless amalgam of tundra and rock, beaten by winds and beaded snow pellets. Adak, Alaska, is a stark land of snow and wind. Razorback juts inland from the bay and I could see it from my house, but only on rare events of sunshine and still.

On such rare days of calm weather—full sun and sixty-five degrees Fahrenheit—a Sunshine Holiday was declared. Workers were released from their duties and children released from school. High schoolers, we flocked together and lay in the sun like the sea lions that lounged, in any weather, on the rocky south side of the remote island. With such seemingly silly criteria as no wind and sunshine for declaring a holiday, it may sound like Adak was a land of leisure, but quite the opposite: I recall conditions for a Sunshine Holiday occurring only twice in the three years I lived there.

It was a great place for me to spend my formative years. I grew to love the outdoors and its inhabitants. I grew to love the rush of blasts of wind and rain. My face pelted by little pellets of snow known as graupel, I felt alive, defiant of the environment that was trying to kill me. I developed a nascent bond with another species that inhabited the challenging environment. Adak was a perfect place for ravens.

Ravens are different. When ducks and dickey birds cower in shelter, ravens challenge the wind and the rain, dancing on updrafts and pecking through the sleet. In the worst of weather, they play, reveling in stormy mists.

Ravens swoop from cliff edges and spear into the wind. Wings tucked, they rotate through barrel rolls and dive like black bullets, skimming over rain-soaked tundra. In a sudden explosion of black, they expand their wings and spread their bodies against the gale, which shoots them upward again, where they tuck, roll, and spin. They dart about in rising bursts, climbing invisible steps of air until they level out and caw, resting on the wind, eye level with their colleagues at the top of the hill. Do the swoops of the ravens illustrate joy? Are the two on top of the cliff actually as haughty and unimpressed as their hopping demeanor suggests? Are their caws calls of admiration when one of their flock adds an extra twist to a roll? Is it a dance of sociality?

Bernd Heinrich, in *Mind of the Raven*, describes raven's sky dances as flight parties.[14] Yes. That is surely what they were. The raven flash mobs were like human high school dances, more for learning how to form a social web than for the ostensible dance moves. Through time and dancing, stronger bonds would sometimes develop between the birds. Two would set apart, perching close together, gently preening each other. I had no idea what was going on in those bird brains was so similar to the emotions and abilities developing in my own brain and body.

A teenager, I had my moments of feeling lost and alone in the wilds of Alaska. An isolation and yearning. I wanted the freedom and exuberance the ravens exhibited. I wanted to caw loudly, to fly and express myself, but to also have friends at the edge of the precipice cheering and jeering playfully. I wanted to be different from the conformist others while fitting in perfectly to my own social group. I saw no irony in it.

My father was straightlaced, Catholic, career Navy; I had to distance myself from that. My friends and I wore our hair long, fussing over it the way the ravens ruffled and preened their feathers. I was flannelled and outdoorsy. Most of my other schoolmates were indoorsy basketball players or cheerleaders. We tolerated each other enough, but spent so much of our energy trying to find a group to fit into. Everyone doing that simultaneously created fission and fusion dynamics that would frustrate the most complicated of mathematical models. My friends and I couldn't help the draw of being collectively different from all the others, those who had sold out or bought in.

Things don't change much after growing up. After achieving middle age in a small town and observing the bickering and gossip and positioning of being seen at or throwing the best parties and events, imagine how saddened I was to discover that high school never ends.

This is all to say that humans can learn a lot about ourselves by zoomorphizing, seeing ourselves as we study the animals. We can learn a lot about how we, as individuals, should and can get along with each other by seeing how—and why—other animals do it. It is the interior battle within teenagers that we ought to be more cognizant of. At that age, their personalities are solidifying, as are the final aspects of their reproductive capabilities. Teenagers are determining if they are social, and how social, by determining who is cool and who's not.

How aggressive or social individuals are within a group defines the group's aggregate personality. Leaders, born or made, create dynamics, changing the cultures and exploits of entire groups. Waves of complexity, emergent properties form when one scales up a level from the individual and examines the effects of multiple individuals forming a group. I've embraced becoming an asocial wildlife biologist, but I've also learned, by comparing humans to spiders and cougars and ravens and a myriad of other species, that for all of humanity's bickering and nastiness, we actually get along more than we don't. Believe it or not, it's within us to cooperate.

CHAPTER 6

Wayfarer or Wallflower

A God-poster sky. The sun shined in beams from cumulous clouds to ocean, spotlights lovingly illuminating waves. The city of Lisbon was poised over the Atlantic. Overlooking the vastness of sand and sea and sunset, I found myself questioning what rested in the distance. Pondering the endless ocean in early evening creates feelings of both boundless hope and trepidation. I thought of what seemed like a gruelingly long flight across the waters and could not imagine the hardships of those ancients who had sailed over wine-dark seas in wooden buckets.

What type of person would it have taken to board the *Niña*, *Pinta*, or *Santa Maria*? Columbus and his intrepid explorers sailing to the west to find the east. Who were the individual Mongols, Romans, and Vikings that swept across the continents and seas, exploring and conquering?

Musing over the fading light on the horizon, I contrasted the dreams of rolling ocean with the solid dependency of land rising behind me. There was more to the collision of water and sand than twilight beauty; down the beach from me turrets and cupolas had been carved from blocks of limestone. The Belém Tower has jutted into the Tagus River since 1519, five stories high, cannons guarding the entrance to Lisbon. Where the sea was a symbol of exploration, the tower was the figure of homeland. They represented the personality types of the wandering wayfarer dispersing to new lands and the homebody wallflower who is more comfortable on familiar ground.

The choice of boat or castle actually constitutes a life strategy for a much broader swath of the earth's creatures than those growing up on Portugal's coast.

In 2007, Else Fjerdingstad, with the Laboratoire d'Ecologie in the Université Pierre et Marie Curie in Paris, wrote what is perhaps the coolest paper that no one has ever heard of. Fjerdingstad and her coauthors studied the simplest of life-forms and produced a paper that provides a basis for observations about personalities at the single-cell scale.[1] The subject of their research was a unicellular, ciliated protozoan called *Tetrahymena thermophile*. The little protists are covered with hairlike cilia, which they use to propel themselves around petri dishes and freshwater ponds. They are microscopic hunters, roaming the pools to forage for bacteria and dissolved nutrients. At 0.002 inches (60 micrometers) long, a few could line up on a human hair.

T. thermophile reproduce mostly by cloning themselves, splitting apart as most single-cell organisms do. They can however, reproduce sexually through a process called conjugation, where two unrelated individuals (clones can't mate with each other) join and exchange their two halves of genetic material. What causes them to pursue sexual reproduction instead of the efficient cloning process? Stress. If conditions in their pool are questionable, such as a shortage of food, *T. thermophile* reproduce by creating one new individual through combining two. The reason they do it, and indeed the reason for sexual reproduction in the first place, is that combining genetic material produces novel variations on biological themes. New amalgams create different individuals with individual variation not present in the parent population. If you are a *T. thermophile*, you can't change the environment, but if conditions are looking bleak, by adding a spice of variation through sexual reproduction you can change your progeny to be better adapted, you hope, to current conditions than you are.

Such events are occasional, but they occur often enough for *T. thermophile* that lines of different types of individuals exist within any population. They may be small, but when looked at closely, it is clear they are not all the same. Some *T. thermophile* are more or less average size and shape, but others become elongated, with more propelling cilia. Some grow a taillike caudal flagellum for extra pro-pulsion. If you watch them closely, it is also clear that they do not all behave the same either. Some individuals become rapid-moving explorers and disperse far and wide, moving four to five times faster through pools than the slowpokes. Others opt for a defensive strat-egy. They work with others of like behavioral temperament to form aggregations; they secrete substances that physically bond their so-cial group together into a walled fort.

In their experiments, Fjerdingstad and colleagues grew several strains of *T. thermophile* under a variety of environmental conditions. Sometimes there were pools of plenty, and other times the colonies were kept on starvation rations. The researchers then watched how the different colonies—cultures of explorers or homebodies—grew. They determined what densities were achieved under each environ-mental condition by each strain. To make the test tubes be more like real life, they also connected the home pool with a small escape tube to new pastures.

In summary, the types of *T. thermophile* that "chose" to be home-bodies were smaller of stature and slower moving, but they could achieve greater densities with equivalent, limited resources. In the words of the researchers, the homebody cells relied more on each other cooperatively and had "stronger sociality." Thus, when things are good, homebodies are favored. When densities were high and starvation was setting in, fast moving strains could successfully make the trek to escape and survive. It may seem that we're stretching the idea of personality by assigning it to a single-celled, ciliated clone, but the fundamental importance of acknowledging the variability between morphology and behavior, even with such "simple" organ-isms is the point. It is just a matter of degree to step to more complex behaviors and life-forms.

Which is where the science becomes a little more complicated. Until now, I have parsed animals into categories based on their bellicosity, appetites, and sociality. One does not have to move to species much more complicated than single-celled organisms, however, to realize that no one—animal or human—is unidimen-sional, falling only into the categories used so far. In truth, singu-lar personality traits create emergent properties. Combined, whole new categories of animals are described. For an organism to be an intrepid explorer, for instance, may take a little more bravery or more comfort in being alone, or some special sauce of traits that creates a wayfarer. Studying how all the different measurable traits interrelate to create explorers, homebodies, or other personality-types-as-lifestyles is the next step in building a more thorough knowledge of animal personality and for understanding how multiple personality traits dance with natural selection.

The field of study about animal personality was coalescing by 2010, when Julien Cote, working with Andrew Sih and other coauthors, composed an excellent overview of the personality traits associated with the wayfaring individuals of many species.[2] Cote and colleagues found certain trends in the types of animals that tend to disperse from their home group. Certain mole rats (*Heterocephalus glaber*) and common lizards (*Lacerta vivipara*) couldn't sit still. Also, some male house mice (*Mus musculus*) were antsier and more likely to disperse. Another hint at the upcoming examination of nature versus nurture, the male wanderers passed on their disposition for movement to their sons.

The confidence that resulted in an individual's tendency to disperse was linked to other measurable traits too. For example, Trinidad killifish (*Rivulus hartii*) that had higher individual boldness scores dispersed farther than their more timid conspecifics. Little short-tailed meadow voles, *Microtus pennsylvanicus*, that dispersed were more aggressive than the others. Aggressive rhesus macaques (*Macaca mulatta*) disperse earlier too. As we will see when we return to bluebirds, the link between aggressiveness and the traveler type can have rather significant repercussions, especially when a foe resides in their new homeland.

Why is animal dispersal relevant? Considering natural selection, what benefits could a lizard receive if it disperses before all the others when its neighborhood becomes packed? In short, an individual's journey may be risky, but if it ends up in a new environment without competitors, it's akin to finding gold at the end of a rainbow.

Nowhere is the jackpot effect more evident than with invading conquerors, invasive species: fire ants, Asian longhorned beetles, emerald ash borers, brown tree snakes, and so many more. What is it about these animals that allows them to invade and take over new habitats? To examine part of that question, Julien Cote and colleagues used a model species, the mosquitofish (*Gambusia affinis*).[3]

The researchers' basic question was to determine if personality-dependent dispersal could fuel the profound abilities of invasive species in ecosystems. Is it just that one species is lucky and outcompetes another, or are certain individuals within a species better at establishing the beachhead?

Mosquitofish were given a bit of an advantage, being introduced to aquatic systems worldwide for the control of mosquitoes. But the fish have been doing exceedingly well in their new homes and have expanded to more than forty countries. They make the top-one-hundred list of invasive species worldwide.

Holding 240 fish in aquaria, Cote put the fish through their behavioral paces, trying to first determine if personality in the little invasive species was demonstrable. Specifically, the researchers wanted to know if the tendency to disperse through experimental streams they created was related to the fishes' other personality traits, such as sociality, braveness or boldness, and activeness and exploration. The researchers needed to measure multiple facets of each animal, and to do it through time. The scientists wanted to be certain about the consistency in personality of the fish—not that some were just feeling adventurous when measured the first time.

To measure how bold or brave a fish was, the researchers relied on methods that we've become familiar with already. Specifically, they put each piscine subject into a small, darkened cylinder that opened into a larger, novel tank and measured the amount of time it took each fish to leave the cover of the darkened cylinder and swim around. And then, after it left, they used cameras to record how much the fish explored the new environment.

How social was each fish? For that question the researchers used a tank partitioned into three sections, a large one in the middle and two smaller ones on either side. A fish put into the middle section could see through the clear partitions but not swim into the other side. Cote and colleagues created a shoal of fourteen mosquitofish in one of the side partitions and left the other side empty. They brought in the subject, who had the choice of hanging out on the party side of the aquarium or retreating to the isolated side. Then the investigators just recorded where each subject fish preferred to hang out.

Having measures of sociality, boldness, and activity for each, they could then examine how a fish's personality type on those axes influenced its decision to disperse along a simulated stream. To distinguish the fish for that experiment, the scientist first gave each fish a unique tattoo by injecting yellow, orange, blue, or red ink into the base of its tail. Then they dumped the ornate fish into a complex of pools separated by raceways of ripples. Fish were given twenty-four hours to decide whether to live in the home pool or to disperse. At the end of the day, the researchers scooped up each fish and determined whether it was a wayfarer or a wallflower.

The personality measures showed that fish who were brave and bold also tended to be more active animals, but the sociality of a fish wasn't strongly correlated to the other tendencies. That is, bold and active fish were both social and asocial. The personality types were unrelated to the physical size and condition of the fish too, so the results were truly due to differences in behavior between the fish and not an effect of physique.

But which fish actually became dispersers? Which other personality traits were linked to a fish's wanderlust? Were they the active fish or the asocial fish? It is interesting that the brave, active fish were not the ones that moved the most through the system of pools and riffles but rather the asocial fish. The more likely a fish was to hang out alone rather than stay close to the other fish, the more likely it would end up in the last pool of the simulated stream. The results were consistent too, because when researchers repeated the tests after a three-week hiatus, the choices made and distances moved the second time were similar to the first time.

Scientists still don't have enough information to compare the behavioral traits of all invasive species with harmonious native species, but layers of personality create a successful invader, because the interplay between asocial and aggressive tendencies within individuals is a primary factor that allows some species to expand and overtake others. The invasive nature of mosquitofish, for example, is likely linked not only to their unique ability to survive in a variety of environments but also to the structure of their "society." That is, by having some animals in a population that seek new environments, the fish are able to constantly find new places to invade and colonize, but they all don't continue to disperse; groups of individuals remain to hold the beachhead when the explorers wander. It's a successful combination.

———

Are some species built to be invasive? It appears so, and nowhere has personality type and ability to invade and conquer been better examined than in bluebirds. We previously saw that some of Renée Duckworth's western bluebirds were aggressive fighters, battling it out over territories to the extent that they failed to spend enough quality time with their mates and young. In the game of genes, the lovers won out over the fighters, but there is more to the story. It's not only the lover versus fighter axis that leads to bluebird happiness. What was the reason fighters were still in a population if they weren't that good at successfully raising young? The answer has to do with the dynamics of ecosystems.[4] Another fiction from which I've been awakening is the "balance of nature." Natural systems and the species that compose them don't, however, rest on an invisible fulcrum barely tipping to one side or another. In actuality, as with bluebird populations, the scales tip completely back and forth frequently and cyclically: and nature's ride is a roller coaster, not an ebbing and flowing tunnel of love.

Let's examine the cycle of a western American forest where bluebirds live. A forest grows and matures. Trees are attacked by insects and age and perhaps a drought. Cavities for nests abound. At that point it is Nirvana for bluebirds. Eventually, however, lightning strikes and the old, dead, and dry wood the birds use for nesting burns. All is reduced to ash, fireweed, and postfire leafy green plants. The bluebirds must find other places to homestead for the next century or so. But the seed bank exists, and soon (in nature's time frame) trees grow back. They mature. Insects and woodpeckers drill the holes that become nesting cavities. In the young ecosystem, a cousin to western bluebirds, mountain bluebirds, are the first to set up shop. There are some snags and nest cavities in the trees, but the conditions are not the best for western bluebirds, which do a little better in older stands. The young stands create a perfect, peaceable kingdom for mountain bluebirds.

As the forest ages, however, it becomes more attractive to western bluebirds. Who will discover the attractive, mature forest that is ripe for invasion by westerns? Explorers, of course. But there is another catch. When the explorers arrive to the new world, someone is already there. The western bluebirds can use the habitat only if they drive out the occupying mountain bluebirds.[5]

Duckworth's explanation is that like a Mongol horde, western bluebirds have been flying across the west, invading the spaces previously occupied by mountain bluebirds. The question is, how do they do it? That western bluebirds are specialists best adapted for the older forests is a source of theoretical confusion. The theory indicates that a species good at dispersing should be good at living in a wide variety of environments, because by dispersing, it can find itself having to live anywhere. It's like a choice between having a good offense or a good defense in most sports. The widely dispersing species will offensively move into and exploit more places, but a species that is uniquely suited for a particular environment should defensively outcompete invasive generalists in that environment.[6]

As so often happens in science, however, elegant and simple theory contrasts with observations of what actually occurs in nature. Duckworth continued her studies of western bluebirds in the Montana woods by marking birds and observing them for three seasons. She employed her usual method of using a tree swallow to taunt the western bluebirds or keeping an innocent bystander house finch in a cage in order to rate each male bluebird for aggressiveness. Recording each western bluebird's temperament and skill at being a good husband and dad, Duckworth then measured how much food he provided for his brooding mate. Ultimately, she could examine which bird, aggressive or not, was the most successful at producing offspring.[7]

In her results, aggressive males were equally aggressive to other bluebirds and competing species, which explains how western bluebird invaders kick the homebody mountain bluebirds' butts. That particular observation, in the context of other personality measurements, was essential for understanding how the system functions. As with mosquitofish, personality traits in bluebirds are also linked—and in a way that favors certain birds in certain circumstances. The traits build on each other: a bird can be a strong wayfarer and explorer, but to be a good invader it must also be an aggressive fighter. Those are the birds that can take over new ground, tipping the ecological scales to establish a beachhead. Duckworth's observations elucidate that there is evolutionary pressure to be an aggressive explorer because the aggressive fighters win the new nest sites, essentially owning the new lands. An apparently clear winner from a natural selection point of view, aggressive explorers, one could predict, would grow to dominate populations. But the homebodies, with their peacenik ways, remain in the populations. Why don't aggressive birds dominate?

To find out, Duckworth tweaked the system by installing nest boxes in new habitats and measured the personalities of the animals that colonized them. As predicted, the explorers were the aggressive conquerors that most successfully colonized a new territory.[8] However, once established in a new area, with all the competing species kicked out, the conditions transformed. By establishing new colonies, the wayfarers ironically created stable colonies just like the colonies that Duckworth examined initially.

Christiaan Both, of the University of Groningen, in 2005, was interested in a line of research paralleling Duckworth's. How do behaviors that are passed down benefit the young?[9] What are the costs and benefits to survival and reproduction if a bird is a brave and aggressive conqueror? Both's team spent four years studying great tits in the wild. They captured individuals and held them for a short period to do the room exploration tests similar to Quinn's (chapter 4) and other authors' approaches. That is, to measure exploring tendencies, the researchers put each bird in a sealed room alone with five artificial trees for perches and measured how actively each bird explored the new surroundings. With data from 225 birds, the study was powerful. The researchers determined that the tendency toward bold and brave exploration influenced nest success and fledgling size and condition. The homebody females had higher nest success and produced the largest fledglings—definitely a benefit.

What about the males' contributions? Opposites may not only attract but the vigor of the variability they instill in their young is also hugely beneficial; the paired parents with either extreme of the behavioral spectrum produced fledglings in the best condition, which led to the highest nest success. Equivalent to Duckworth's research, in Both's study the wayfaring explorers were less social and better able to obtain and conquer high quality territories, but the homebodies were more attentive parents. Each strategy has benefits and costs, and against the backdrop of the real world, it leads to maintenance of intraspecific genetic variation in personality; opposites attract, ensuring diversity.

The system, then, first favors the wayfaring explorers who sweep like a horde through new lands. But because these individuals don't get along with others as well and spend more time fighting than caring for their mates and young, they become less successful at producing young than the homebody birds, who also tend to be the lovers we saw in chapter 3. Due to combined effects of multiple personality traits, explorers are selected against as the colony becomes a stable and aging population, which further contributes to the stability of the population.

Thus, the ecology of a species, and the battles between them, can be driven by differences in behavior between individuals within populations. What this means is that animal personality is not just a quaint phenomenon of intriguing differences between individuals. It means that personality, as measured in individuals, creates emergent properties and interplay that build into societies and structures that actually drive ecological systems. The personality of a population—its culture—is honed by environmental pressures too. All the examples of evolution, such as the specialized beaks on Darwin's finches in the Galapagos, aren't the whole story. Individual variation in behavior, as measured by personality type, is as important as physiology in ecology and evolution.

CHAPTER 7

Nature and Nurture

Niels J. Dingemanse, another powerhouse in the study of animal personality, does much of his research on great tits.[1] In one of his team's papers, he investigated whether dispersal of young birds correlated with their personality type. Specifically, he and his collaborators caught wild birds and tested them for their degree of exploratory behavior in novel environments. Like the other studies, the researchers captured the birds, tested their behavioral tendencies, and then released them to see which birds tended toward dispersal and which didn't. To measure exploring tendencies, Dingemanse and colleagues put each bird in a sealed room alone with five artificial trees for perches. The brave birds would hop between and among all the perches and the timid birds would not. What propelled the science forward, however, was not just determining once again that different birds had different personalities, but that Dingemanse knew the lineages of the birds: the investigators were able to measure the personality of the parents and then correlate their behaviors with the dispersal strategy of their young.

Put simply, the researchers were asking if exploring parents tend to raise young that also explore and disperse. As in many other studies, they measured the physical attributes of the young birds and found no correlations between how far the birds dispersed after fledging and their weight, size, or hatching date. Again, the physical attributes weren't the predictors of each bird's life strategy. The researchers did demonstrate, however, that the young of brave and exploring parents dispersed farther and the female young especially moved more in their journeys.

An argument about the role of genes versus the role of the environment, nature versus nurture, continues, but Dingemanse's studies showed that genetics do indeed play an important role in the development of personality. Continued research by Pieter Drent at the Netherlands Institute of Ecology elegantly quantified the relationship between genetics and personality type. He demonstrated, like Dingemanse, that the tendency toward brave and bold exploration was conserved from parent to offspring.[2] Using breeding trials, Drent determined that genetics were responsible for more than 50 percent of an animal's brave, exploring tendencies. By handing down the wanderlust literally in their genes, great cultures of explorers can develop, be they great tits or Great Britain.

Kayla Sweeney, working with Jonathan Pruitt's lab at the University of Pittsburgh, studied the grass spider *Agelenopsis pennsylvanica*. Spiders of this genus are the ones that create the flat webs that appear in morning dew on mowed grass. Theirs is a complicated world of predator, prey, and personality playing out daily in the jungles of suburban lawns. Sweeney assessed the development of aggressive foraging and boldness in her study subjects.[3]

Studying her paper, I was reminded that another reason the science of animal personality may not be as familiar to the lay public as it should be is the alien language that scientists often use. Sweeney and her colleagues' research is fascinating and quite relevant to both two- and eight-legged creatures, but the professional journals are filled with incomprehensible geek speak. For example, Sweeney assessed "the roles of correlated selection and divergent rearing environments in generating a syndrome." The researchers determined that their data were (spoiler alert) "consistent with the hypothesis that the boldness-aggressiveness syndrome exhibited by wild *A. pennsylvanica* develops as a result of environmentally induced phenotypic plasticity, and not correlated selection."[4]

In layperson's terms, Sweeney and colleagues collected spiders from urban hedgerows in Pennsylvania and gave them boxes to live and spin webs in. The investigators then ran the spiders through some tests to see how they differed in personality and how their rearing environment influenced how they acted later in life. They fasted each arachnid for three days and then dropped a two-week-old cricket into its web and timed how long it took for the spiders to attack the prey. Their inference, along with that of many other researchers, was that a lower latency to attack meant a higher degree of aggressiveness, a tendency toward a predatory personality. Spiders can be prey too, so the researchers assessed the spiders' braveness in the face of a potential threat. Testing the prey response with spiders is much easier than with packs of wolves or coyotes; instead of requiring large pens and long strips of fabric, it requires an infant ear-cleaning bulb. To startle a spider, the researchers sneaked up behind the eight-legged lord of the flies and puffed two bursts of air, which caused the spider to flee, curl up in its web, and hide. The time it took for a spider to return was the measure of its bravery, its ability to laugh at the face of death, to treat threats with aplomb rather than with the personality of a timorous prey.

Sweeney and her team also examined the interplay between nature and nurture by capturing and testing the spiders, and then marking and releasing them. That way Sweeney could measure spider personality as they aged in a natural, variable environment. Brilliantly, Sweeney and colleagues also bred generations of spiders and raised them in identical plastic cups, an unvarying and austere environment in contrast to the natural world.

Individual wild-living spiders, as we've come to expect, tended toward either being more brave and predatory or being more timid and defensive. Tracking the spiders through time, the scientists concluded what we've seen in so many other species too: as young spiders got older, their aggressive and bold traits softened and they were less willing to attack and less willing to return to forage after being intimidated by an air puff. Spiders raised in the laboratory under simplified conditions, however, did not show the same correlations between aggressiveness and boldness in individuals. Living in plastic cups, they were less variable, and the simplified environments brought out the genetic basis of their personalities. The researchers determined that daily variation shaped wild spiders to be more cautious in general. Were their results that the environment created spider personality in contrast to the gene-based observations of researchers such as Dingemanse? Has the argument of nature versus nurture been resurrected? What are the roles of genes and the environment?

———

We've seen examples of dolphins getting PTSD from environmental influences and spider populations settling toward bland uniformity when raised under austere conditions, but we've also observed the heritability of personality traits through generations. How are we to sort out the order and importance of nature and nurture?

The answer of how to frame our understanding comes from an influential paper by Theodosius Dobzhansky, a geneticist and evolutionary biologist who in 1973 set the tone for animal behavioral studies when he asserted that "nothing in biology makes sense except in the light of evolution"[5] Simply, evolution cannot occur without the process of natural selection, which cannot occur without variation and heritability. Variation in behavior between individuals is personality; heritability is what is carried by genes.

Richard Dawkins, in his accessible and important book *The Selfish Gene*, masterfully explains how, and at what level, natural selection and evolution function.[6] Dawkins teaches that a gene is just a bit of coding that provides instructions for building a protein. The genome is essentially the blueprint for the frameworks of proteins that create bodies, including the neural networks that create behavior.

Life is a tricky term to define, but at a minimum, life is the process of self-replicating a biochemical bundle. The essential bundle, in Dawkins's view, is the gene, because it contains the information that is replicated at the most fundamental biochemical level. What Dawkins did was confront the notion that animals create genes in order to replicate themselves. Instead, he argued that the opposite is true: genes produce organisms to replicate themselves. Through this lens, individuals, families, species, and societies are essentially a means to a gene's end. Any biological organism is impermanent and transient, but the genes that create them are nearly immortal. You are your genes' host, serving their benefit, but if you don't reproduce,

they don't; so the magic and wonder resides in the mutually beneficial relationship we animals have with our genes.

Natural selection, in its most basic form, is the process of ending
the lines of some genes while allowing others to replicate. If one line
codes for characteristics that are beneficial in a particular environment, such as being a brave explorer, then that line will continue.
What is most fascinating, however, as we've begun to see in bluebirds and tits, is that nature selects genes for precise characteristics
in the short term, but selects for a wide array of diversity in the long
run. This interplay between genes, the environment, and the web
of individual variation that is expressed as personality is the topic of
investigation in this chapter.

———

Claudio Carere's work at the University of Groningen is a prime
example of the advances in the study of individual variation and animal personality that are originating in the Netherlands.[7] Carere and
colleagues used the familiar European favorite, the great tit, to examine how consistent personality types were in the little birds. They
hatched their birds at the Centre for Terrestrial Ecology, Heteren,
and tested the tits as young juveniles (fewer than two months old)
and as adults.

Similar to other experiments, the researchers first determined
if individual birds were hesitant and cautious or quick to actively
explore a novel room. Next, the investigators confronted each male
with an intruder male and measured how aggressive the subject was.
Finally, the scientists examined sexual preferences by putting a male
or female in a cage next to two other cages that each housed a bird
of the opposite sex. Preference was a simple matter of recording
which potential mate the researchers' subject spent the most time
with. Testing the birds repeatedly, Carere and colleagues measured
exploratory behavior for individuals through time. They measured
aggression twice in adult birds, with a seven-month lag between measurements, and then put it all in the context of adult sexual behavior.

The tits fell into groups of bold and fast or shy and slow. The
"fast explorers" were aggressive, bold in exploration, insensitive to
external stimuli, and relied on routines; they were something akin to

ESTJ in the Myers-Briggs framework. They were the "born great" type in Shakespeare's schema. The "slow explorers" were more passive, less aggressive, shy, sensitive to external stimuli, and adjusted their actions depending upon their environment. They were like the wallflowers at a preteen dance, taking longer than the fast explorer jocks to approach a member of the opposite sex. The shy ones were like INTPs, or the "have greatness thrust upon them" types of birds.

Bird personalities remained consistent but were shaped by time. Birds did not flip-flop or become someone entirely different, but some of them, especially the homebodies, became braver and bolder as they got older—albeit not as bold as the bold birds. The bold birds didn't change as much and were more or less equivalent in behavior whether they were young or old.

Another element of their experiments, the topic of this chapter, is that Carere and colleagues had actually cheated a little. That is, the experimental subjects they used were the result of artificial selection. Before the experiment, the researchers had been selectively breeding the birds for or against being explorers. They paired explorers with explorers for four generations and used them as the subjects. Indeed, by choosing from the different genetic lines, the researchers produced young explorer birds seven to eight times faster at exploring novel situations than the homebody line.

The researchers asked the question that we've been caroming by in this book until now: Is it nature or nurture that causes animals to have a certain personality type? By showing that the birds could be bred for certain personality traits, the researchers showed that there is indeed a genetic component to personality. But how much mind control are genes responsible for?

How can the influence of genes on a trait, such as the tendency to be a bold explorer, be measured? Measuring the role of genes using breeding trials is often done to produce an estimate of *heritability*. Heritability, to put it as simply as possible, is the measure of the variability of a trait in a population due to genetics versus the environment. For a simple example, let's consider a person's height. If it was completely determined by the nutrition they received as children, heritability would be zero. A child receiving starvation rations while growing would be very short as an adult, and one with full nutrition would become exceedingly tall. In contrast, if everyone was exactly the same height no matter what they ate growing up, then heritability would be 1.0, or 100 percent. In actual fact, we are pre-programmed to be close to our parents' heights, but environmental factors such as nutrition influence whether or not we fulfill or exceed our genetic potential. Behavior is a result of both a genetic map and an environmental influence. For great tits and exploratory behavior, as it turns out, the heritability of the explorer behavior is 54 percent. That is, 54 percent of the variation in explorer behavior is caused by genes and 46 percent by the environment. Thus, scientists have by-passed the red herring trail leading to a dichotomy between nature and nurture; instead, they have begun to quantify both, sometimes working for years and with dozens of generations to identify where genetic control ends and environmental influence begins.

The most famous breeding experiment designed to create a personality type from a wild animal used Russian foxes, which were bred for their docility by Russian scientist Dmitry K. Belyaev. Belyaev started a breeding program in the 1950s and continued the lines until his death in 1985.[8] The work is the subject of much press and is worthy of exploration in itself, if for no other reason than the tame foxes are exceedingly cute. At the Institute of Cytology and Genetics at Novosibirsk, Belyaev sought to mimic an evolutionary pathway toward domesticated animals. His test subjects were dark, melanistic versions of the red fox that had been bred for generations at a farm. The project continues today, run by a former intern, Lyudmila Trut.

The researchers selected foxes through time, not for their fur but rather for how the animals responded when their cage was opened. Most foxes were naturally wary and favored running away to escape, but about 10 percent of them displayed a weak "wild-response." That is, a small proportion of animals were confident and docile around humans. Trut was selecting for the characteristics of friendlier and tolerant to human touch, even to a small degree, in order to determine if and when aggressiveness and fear could be eliminated from the captive fox population. Those that hid in the corner or made aggressive vocalizations were excluded from the breeding experiments.

From the friendly foxes, one hundred vixens and thirty males were chosen as the first generation of parents. Under such precise selection, changes in behavior and physiology became pronounced quickly. By the fourth selected generation, pups were responding to humans with doglike tail wagging.[9] With each generation, the off-spring continued to be more like domestic dog pets, and by the sixth generation, some foxes wagged their tails, whined, whimpered, and licked like little dog puppies.

How much of a role did genetics play then? A lot. The most do-mestically adorable of pups constituted only 1.8 percent of the popu-lation by the sixth generation, 18 percent by the tenth, and 35 percent by the twentieth generation. The experiment is renowned for its du-ration. By the thirtieth generation, the proportion of domesticated pups grew to 49 percent. Astoundingly, after examining and crossing 10,500 foxes and producing 50,000 offspring, almost all the foxes in the last generations had become like a fox named Martin.

—

Dark ears and eyes fade effortlessly into a silver gray, like wispy fog on a spring morning in Russia. His shimmering coat, luxurious waves of argent fur, beacon me to reach into it, to stroke and pet. Paedo-morphism—the retention of juvenile characteristics in an adult—is enthusiastically demonstrated by Martin in both the puppy-like softness of his face and the fur, but even more so by his fawning demeanor. Martin will happily accept gentle strokes and massages, licking at an offered hand. His inky black nose punctuates a white patch that forms at his forehead, strengthens between his eyes, and broadens over his muzzle. There are a few spots of steeliness above his nose, like the highlights on a blue merle Australian shepherd. He's not a dog, although he fawns and wags his ivory-tipped tail while prancing on white socks like the happiest of irresistible pup-pies. Martin, as reported by the television program *Russia Today*, lives in a Moscow flat with Larisa Rosanov.[10]

Breeding the Russian foxes purely on behavioral characteris-tics hints at another important result of the genetic malleability of personality: "man's best friend." Our eyes feast on the exceptional physical variety of dogs, from little Chihuahuas to Irish wolfhounds, but our hearts depend upon the smiles, licks, and cuddles of the domestic dog temperament. What do Belyaev's foxes show us about how humans created our domestic dogs? Were cavemen stealing the friendliest pups from litters and crossing them for fifty years until we had Gretchens or Martins? Yes, and no, because the choice to create a bond between human and wolf requires more than a human's decision. The dogs undoubtedly played a role too.[11] That is, we didn't just choose them. The dogs that were comfortable around humans also chose us; they made the self-selecting choice that began a mutualistic collaboration between species. Human and dog formed the alliances due to their abilities to reach out and bond and cooperate with another individual. The dogs that were best at bonding with humans became our domestic breeds. The wary and aloof dogs are still around too. They are called wolves.

Research into how genes and the environment influence the manifestation of personality continues, including studies of our European friend, the great tit. A familiar name and prodigious researcher, Niels Dingemanse, along with his colleagues, continues to expand previous research on great tits by investigating how personality types survive through time.[12] In one study, they were interested in understanding how the environment influenced the survival and reproduction of the various personality types. The scientists captured the great tits from the Westerheide population in the Netherlands and used the experimental design that we have become familiar with: releasing birds into a novel room with perches to test how aggressive an explorer each bird was. The investigators gave each bird an individual numbered ring for identification and then released it, letting nature take its course for three years.

What was the effect of being an explorer? It depended. In 1999 and 2001, it was great to be a bold female, as the explorer females survived much better than their timid counterparts. In 2000, however, the explorer females had a terrible year. Many of them died. The reverse was true for males, as survival was very low for explorer males in 1999 and 2001, but extremely high in 2000. Survival and, indeed, reproduction were related to environmental conditions and the personality of the individual, but what was the cause of the correlation?

Food. Specifically beech seeds. Beech trees vary in how well they reproduce every year. Some years they produce a large nut crop, which can provide food for the tits, and other years the birds are left famished.

The researchers postulated that 1999 and 2001 were poor winters, without an abundance of beech mast. The opposite was true the winter of 2000, when there was lots of nutritious food. During years with good beech crops the competition for food lessens and more young survive—which creates more competition for territories the following year.

The effect is to create different pressures on males and females, because the great tit breeding system relies on females being subordinate to males and not vying for territory space themselves. The females are most directly affected by competition for food, and the homebodies focus better on fattening themselves and their young when food is abundant, while the explorers do better when food is scarce and needs to be searched for. The males, however, have different and opposite pressures. The males' prime duty is to obtain and defend territories, and thus they are more affected by competition for territories. In essence, the aggressive explorer males benefit in poor resource years by outcompeting their humble competitors, and the homebody females do better in the rich years, taking full advantage of nature's abundance. A changing environment means that no one bird type always wins.[13]

Scientists are now discovering interplay between personalities, the environment, and genetics everywhere they look. Denis Réale and his coauthors, for example, studied a wild Canadian population of bighorn sheep and how different personality types of ewes led to different competitive benefits in different situations.[14] To capture sheep, the researchers baited corrals with salt blocks, which attracted the nutrient-seeking sheep. The corral full, the researchers slammed the door and jumped in to grab sheep by the horns, blindfold them, and immobilize them with leg hobbles. While held thus, technicians checked on the health, weight, and reproductive status of each ewe, evident by the fullness of their udders.

Knowing something about the physical aspects of the sheep, the scientists also described behavioral aspects. The first behavioral attribute the scientists measured was boldness, which we've been typically thinking of as bravery. Specifically, the researchers measured each ewe's willingness to leave their accustomed cover and enter the corral trap. Some bold animals rushed in without any hesitation. Shy animals approached more slowly and entered and exited several times before they tentatively approached the bait. For a measure of docility, the researchers created a score based on how aggressively captured ewes fought back against their human muggers. It was something like a cowboy calf-roping scale: if the ewe lay down by herself when caught, she got zero points, but she earned one point if she resisted. Depending upon how much effort it took to wrestle the trapped ewe, she received zero to two points. She got another zero to one point for how hard it was to keep her down, zero to one for the difficulty to hog-tie her, and zero to two for struggling while being moved. Subtracting the earned score from seven, a ewe was most docile with a score of seven, and the most obstreperous with a score of zero.

Using several years of capture data and observations, the researchers could clearly see that different ewes differed consistently in their degree of boldness. The heritability they calculated for the trait was 0.21; that is, 21 percent of the variation in bold personality was due to genetics. Docility was also highly repeatable for individuals within and between years. Some ewes just gave up, and others were aggressive fighters. Interestingly, and very important in the game of genes, there was a weak negative correlation between docility and boldness. Bold ewes tended toward being aggressive fighters too. No ewes were both timid to enter and aggressive in their fighting style.

Over time, bold ewes, at first examination, were the natural selection winners. They explored more and took advantage of new resources faster, so they reproduced at an earlier age than shy ewes. In better physical shape because of their behavioral choices, they had a higher weaning success too.

Then the rules changed when the mountain lions moved in. Suddenly predation was intense, and bravely venturing away from

the safety of exposed rocks—where a ewe could see a predator coming—became a horrendous liability. The tendency for certain ewes
to fight back didn't matter, providing no defense to the ambush attack of the cougars. The appetite versus appetizer balance reversed
on the sheep, and the formerly well-fed became the food. Because
the personality types were heritable, it meant that mountain lions
could have an effect on the tendency toward brave and bold aggressive fighters within the population of sheep. The evidence continues
to mount: great tits, bluebirds, bighorn sheep. By selecting both for
and against different personality types through time each year, nature actually ensures that multiple personality types remain within
a population. Nature pressures populations to have a diversity of
personalities and not to create only one uniquely best type. The interplay between genes and natural selection from ever-changing environments means that variation will continue in all species.

Will researchers ever find one particular personality gene? Will they
have to search for teams or armies of genes that control behavior?
Will that even be possible? Some insist that to demonstrate personality most definitively would require a mechanistic description
linking gene to protein to behavior. Researchers have begun focusing on a few genes that at least contribute to an animal's personality.
One example is the dopamine D4 receptor gene, or DRD4, known
to molecular psychiatrists as the "adventure gene."[15] The gene influences the degree of boldness in terms of investigating novelty and
the tendency to be an explorer in a number of vertebrate species.[16]
Variations of DRD4 and its influence on behavior have been found
in domestic chickens, horses, dogs, and captive vervet monkeys, so
the gene deserves focused research.

Peter Korsten and colleagues at the Max Planck Institute for Ornithology in Seewiesen, Germany, for example, wanted to know how
DRD4 varies in different populations separated by miles and oceans.
In their research they sampled great tits from the Netherlands,
Belgium, and the United Kingdom. They tested tits in the way described earlier: capturing individuals from the field and then releasing the little birds into a test chamber to record how they hopped

and moved through the novel environment. In addition to their behavioral observations, Korsten and colleagues obtained blood and
feather samples, which they used for an intensive genetic analysis.

In the Westerheide population from the Netherlands, there was
a positive relationship between DRD4 and the exploratory behavior
of the birds. The other population of great tits in the Netherlands
had a weaker relationship between the gene and the birds' personalities. But what stumped the researchers was that for the birds in
Belgium and the United Kingdom, no relationship between the state
of DRD4 and the birds' personalities existed. For some bird populations, it seems, the gene looked like the key, and then in other
populations it had no effect at all, which is a puzzling discovery, to
say the least. In some populations, one gene can have a big effect on
the personalities of individuals, but the effects are more complicated
because not only is there variation within populations, there is also
variation between populations. Natural selection applies pressure in
multiple ways: some individuals may "win" with the right characteristics at a given time and place, and some populations may outcompete others due to a different blend of individuals.

Zoomorphizing at the gene level, we can see that humans are
again much the same as the other animals: the DRD4 gene also correlates with the exploratory behaviors of humans, but the degree of
association between gene and behavior varies between human populations and is not even found in some populations. The role of the
environment and the influence of multiple genes remain a mystery.
Is there a genetic component to behavior and personality? Yes, absolutely. But will one "explorer" or "shy" gene ever be found or even
a specific suite of genes that dictate an individual's temperament?
Unlikely. The actual interplay between personality and genetics will
provide fodder for many scientific investigations to come.

Obsessive hair pulling occurs in humans, dogs, cats, mice, rats,
guinea pigs, rabbits, sheep, and even musk oxen.[17] In humans the
disorder is called *trichotillomania*, and it affects about 1.5 percent of
men and 3.5 percent of women in the United States. Behaviors can
include plucking hairs from the scalp, eyebrows, eyelashes, beards,

or pubic area. The behavior is often brought on by some form of stress, and the plucking acts like a pressure release.

We may know more about obsessive hair pulling because it occurs in lab animals. Perhaps their surroundings contribute to the behaviors, but the nature of their captivity also means that animal-care staff can watch the animals closely and detect psychological ticks. Mice sometimes become barbers, for instance, not only obsessively washing and nibbling at their own fur with their paws and saliva but also grooming, nibbling, and plucking at the hair of other willing mice.

Shau-Kwaun Chen and colleagues, cellular biologists at the University of Utah, followed a linear and mechanistic path from gene to behavior that would undoubtedly make Renée Duckworth envious.[18] Where Duckworth focused on free-ranging birds responding to natural variation, Chen and colleagues had a closed-circuit system where they could link the clues together to tell a larger story. Chen's research focused on compulsive grooming in mice, specifically those that carried the Hoxb8 gene.

The researchers used floor vibration monitors to record all the activity of the mice in their cages. They saved hundreds of hours of direct human observation and evaluation by using a computer algorithm to translate vibration patterns into the activities the mice were doing: drinking, eating, rearing, climbing, locomotion, immobility, and grooming and scratching. Behaviors were thus mapped without having to disturb or bother the mice at all. They could quantitatively evaluate the amount of overgrooming and measure the resulting bald spots and injuries too.

The first observation about Hoxb8 mice is that they tend to be obsessive groomers, but how does that gene cause such behaviors? The gene codes for a type of cell, called *microglia*, that occurs in the brain and spinal cord, and is an initial line of defense against infection. The Hoxb8 gene functions in bone marrow, where the microglia are created.

To determine what did what, the scientists had control mice that were normal and lab reared, but of no particular genetic lineage (known as "wild type"). Those mice were not prone to overgroom. Other mutant mice did. To determine the mechanism for how the

genes influenced behavior, the scientists did bone-marrow trans-
plants on the different groups of mice. Normal mice that received
normal bone marrow continued to act normally. Mice with Hoxb8
mutation and the hair-pulling compulsion, when given the same type
of bone marrow transplant, continued to obsessively groom. Two of
the ten mice that were normal at first, after being given "defective"
marrow, developed bald patches, and the whole group increased
their grooming behaviors more than the controls.

Can a behavioral disorder be cured with gene therapy?

In the group of Hoxb8 mutant mice that received normal bone
marrow cells, their hairless patches continued to grow for a few
weeks after the transplant, but then, after about three months, six
of the ten subjects showed extensive regrowth of hair in the hairless
areas and healing of their sores. Their grooming times decreased
significantly such that they acted like normal, nonobsessive mice. At
least for one problematic behavioral trait, the researchers found a
specific gene and created a gene therapy that could fix the behavior:
four of the treated mice fully recovered and were indistinguishable
from normal controls. It is a small step, limited to the influence of a
gene on a specific behavior rather than a broad personality type, but
science is inching its way toward resolving the genetic and physiological mechanisms that create our identities.

How genes control bodies and behavior is the question that has determined the path of Renée Duckworth's career. Following the time-
line of her discoveries is delightful. They come together like a good
detective novel, with grand deductions and plot twists and turns.
She first discovered the relationships between aggressive personalities and body types and habitat selection in western bluebirds. From
that, she observed the detrimental effect of aggression: that bellicose
bluebirds were failing at natal care. Poor parenting skills should have
meant that those birds would die out. Resolving the mystery, Duckworth found an interplay between aggression, the environment, and
competition between western and mountain bluebirds—which, of
course, led Duckworth to try to tie together questions about the
proximal causes for behavior, such as hormones, and the ultimate

causes of how evolution shapes gene expression. That is where her notions cross over to other disciplines normally as far apart as a lab mouse and a lodgepole pine.

Evolutionary ecologists typically think in terms of millennia and about *ultimate mechanisms*—the long-term reasons why organisms have been shaped into what they've become. But Duckworth bridges the gap, also describing *proximate mechanisms*—the hormone or gene or specific mechanism that causes an individual's variation. "It's stress," she tells me, "especially stress in utero."[19] Most evolutionary ecologists don't think that way, leaping to a proximate cause with aplomb, but Duckworth is innovative and confident enough to cross disciplines. By broadening her frame of reference, she's benefitted from a breadth of knowledge. She asserts that separate disciplines can take advantage of each other's unique approaches.

"I really think we need to understand the neuroendocrine system . . . on the individual basis." She favors continuing to create and cross bridges and to be open to what scientists have learned about humans. We know things about human brains that we can apply to animals.

I ask about the specter of anthropomorphizing. She says that she remembers being yelled at by her mentors for anthropomorphizing onto cats around the lab, so she has had some experience with reactionary dogma. But after becoming an accomplished scientist, her views solidified. "I feel like a lot of things in science go to one end of the spectrum," she says. In Morgan's day, researchers were probably anthropomorphizing too much. Like every other young scientist that I interviewed, she concluded that since the early times it has gone too far the other way. To say that human brains think and feel differently than all other species, "it denies the evolutionary aspect of behavior." Acknowledging that all minds are different, she asserts, "The challenge is to figure out what is similar." It's a concept she feels passionate about, because the constraints have "inhibited research."

The primary danger of anthropomorphizing is more about the problem of being anthropocentric. "If we put the mind in an evolutionary context, we have to admit that their brains will work similarly to ours," Duckworth says. Science can identify where there are similarities between us and other animals in structure and behavior, but we can't automatically assume that other species experience the world exactly as humans do. There is some balance in the approach. "Scientists can learn a lot about how the brain works by having people sit in an MRI, but normally that can't be done with animals, certainly not wild ones." Duckworth also observes that although evolutionary biologists can learn from psychologists and neurologists, they can learn from the field biologists too. The norm for describing human behavior tends to rely on surveys and self-assessment; Duckworth wonders what we'd learn if we observed humans the way she watched bluebirds. The comparative approach, allowing some latitude in concept and language, would most certainly lead to greater understanding.

Without being asked, she recites a dictionary definition of personality: "'consistent individual variation across time and context.' It's a good operational definition," she continues, "but ultimately my own way of thinking about personality is . . . those traits that are connected to organs and structures are real personality traits." She's searching for an epigenetic holy grail of exactly how genes create personality types. Her current path has her firmly following a trail toward the effects of early development. Specifically, how a mother's stress influences the physiology and behavior of her offspring.

As an example, Duckworth recounts the effects of food shortages in the Netherlands during World War II. At the beginning of the end of the war in Europe, the Germans were punishing the Dutch by banning all food transports to the country.[20] When the embargo was lifted in November 1944, the country was paralyzed by the effects of an early and cold winter. The canals were frozen, and moving food from the rural west to the urban east was impossible. Food supplies ran out, and adults were forced to strict rations. The rationed calories slumped from eighteen hundred per day in 1943 to between four hundred and eight hundred from December 1944 to April 1945. Pregnant and nursing mothers were initially provided extra food, but during the height of the famine, they were being starved too. It wasn't until the liberation of the Netherlands in early May 1945 that relief came.

Using detailed medical records, researchers were able to track the cohort of children who were conceived during the early, middle, and later parts of the famine. Their findings were dramatic. From the 2,414 people they monitored, they determined that those whose mothers were food stressed early in their fetal development experienced more instances of coronary heart disease, obesity, and diabetes.

If a mother is food stressed, then the offspring are primed for a scarce environment, supercharged for sugar, for stressful situations, which has physiological impacts on how the heart works, including how the body processes sugar. The children of the Dutch famine mothers were calibrated for famine but lived in a world of largess. The physiological and behavioral impacts led to obesity, heart disease, and diabetes.

From that study Duckworth reasons that bodies can be primed for an environment, preset for the conditions in which they will likely live. "Genes set the range; the environment sets how the animal will express the genes." The vagaries of gene expression and environmental variability are a game of chance, chaotic aspects of nature and nurture that create an inevitable array of unique individuals.

CHAPTER 8

The Selfish Herd,
the Generous Gene

As we hiked up the 13,061-foot-high Wheeler Peak in Nevada, my fourteen-year-old son asked me why there were so many animals and why there wasn't just one perfect species. I explained that in my mind, he was the apex of evolution and as perfect as they come. After his perfunctory eye roll, we continued our climb. We gained a couple thousand feet of elevation, moving from a mountain meadow into a stand of four-thousand-year-old bristlecone pines. Every step of elevation, the collage of species changed. The firs yielded to scree, but even amid the rocks we saw magnificent flowers and greenery, suckling on drips from remnant snow patches.

Within a fold of mountain, we entered a valley of shade where ice remained long into the summer. On the back of the ridge, however, the sun beat down, sublimating the snow into mist. So much changed with minor traverses from the north to the south side of the mountain. More differences between the thick, desert air of the mountain's base and the rarified thinness on its high peak. So many climates and microclimates literally within meters of each other. It is difficult to think of a species that is best adapted for every spot on the mountain. Even humans, having developed behaviors such as creating clothes, can go everywhere, yet few of us opt to live on mountaintops.

The earth has such a magnificent diversity of life because this is such a marvelous and complicated world. Add to the topographical complexity the vagaries of time, and the complexities multiply. Down to the individual, each species casts its lots against the uncertain environment.

Some physical adaptations confer obvious benefits on a particular environment, like a monkey's prehensile tail or the beaks of Darwin's finches. But bodies transmogrify more slowly than glaciers advance and recede. Behavior, then, allows individuals to adapt and be resilient more quickly than the evolution of purely physical characteristics allows. Such is the microevolutionary importance of behavioral variability and personality. Behavior is more than an ecological afterthought, hitched to physiology. Behavior allows animals to cheat the limitations of their physiologies. What would the costs in energy be for dolphins to grow sponge-like forms to protect their noses, or for New Caledonian crows to create sticklike protuberances out of their beaks to carry as tools? And how many eons would it take? Instead, behavior and learning allow animals to not alter their bodies but to alter how they use their bodies, depending upon environmental changes and needs. A person cannot grow wings, but a few strong personalities with feelings of wonder mixed with innovation and radical and aggressive risk taking are what ultimately allowed the rest of us to fly.

Personalities allow quick responses to ecological vagaries; sometimes the aggressive funnel spiders or great tits win the reproductive challenge. In other conditions they lose. A wolf or coyote in a pack must share, but a pair of explorers can win a jackpot, stumbling into new competition-free, game-filled lands. Fighters can gain territory, but they can also lose it through injury. Aggressive hunters grow large on a bounty of protein, just as bighorn sheep fatten their udders when free of cougars, but if any animal becomes too fearless, their own muscles become meat.

Nature embraces and encourages variation and thrives on difference. What happens when we reject nature's preference?

———

We've done amazing things with chickens. The modern laying hen, for example, is a wonder, prodigiously popping out packets of protein known as eggs.[1] Hens have greatly increased their productivity over their ancestors; during the few decades from 1950 to the early 1990s, egg numbers increased from fewer than 270 to more than 340 eggs per year per hen (a 29 percent increase). As if quantity wasn't enough, during that time, the size of eggs also increased by 42.7 percent.

A seemingly humble experiment on the potential of artificial selection of chickens by William Muir at Purdue University probably caused more of a splash than Muir expected. His research results were adapted into a business model in a highly successful TED talk by Margaret Heffernan.[2] Summarizing Muir's work, Heffernan described the development of a flock of superchickens. The flock was a perfect analog, creating a parable about a company composed of only high-pressured top performers.

In his experiment, Muir kept average chickens in one flock and put only the most productive egg-layers into another flock. The hypothesis was that if a work group was filled, as company managers try to do, with only superproductive individuals, a uniform and superproductive group will be created. Heffernan noted that sort of selection for productivity, creating teams of ideal and dedicated workers, was something most companies, and even some countries, do. The results of Muir's experiment, however, were not intuitive, but they make perfect sense if we apply the lessons of variation and adaptation.

After breeding superchickens for only six generations, the breeding backfired. The problem was not due to the physiological capability of hens to lay eggs but due to a link between physiology and behavior. Like Renée Duckworth's long-tailed and short-tailed bluebirds, elements of personality were being weeded out with the physical selection.

Whenever I watch chickens, I can't help but think of them as little, brutal, cooing dinosaurs. If a grasshopper jumps into their pen, anything cute about the hens evaporates, and they run like velociraptors, shoving and pouncing, tearing the bug to pieces. Their innate aggressiveness comes out in their relationship with each other too. Hen interpersonal skills have become an idiom: they organize themselves through a literal pecking order. I certainly know that Hipster is at the top of the pecking order in my backyard flock, followed by Pepita and Luna.

My chickens have the room of a run and can get around each other so that no serious fights occur, which is not the case in commercial egg-producing operations. With flocks in small spaces, the fights can be extreme. Muir's superchickens, as it turned out, were genetically programmed to be phenomenal layers, but the type-A hens had another problem: after six generations, the layers' personalities were so aggressive that they literally killed each other. By comparison, the flock of average chickens kept laying; they struck a balance between living together in a flock and laying eggs. By the time Muir ended the experiment, only three battle-hardened superchickens were left. The few that remained couldn't possibly produce as much as the average flock.

Muir's research has profound significance for animal welfare. The tragedy caused by the quest after World War II for the most productive egg-layer is that egg farmers had to begin incorporating other unseemly practices into husbandry, such as beak trimming and designing isolated housing. If breeders, however, incorporate the insights of animal personality into their programs and don't select for only one physiological trait, they can raise chickens that are happy, healthy, and productive without having to snip their beaks or impound them.[3]

The parable of the superchicken is not lost on those who have found themselves in the maw of an overbuilt team of top performers. Infighting and aggression will actually slow down innovation. Besides, there isn't only one best type of person or personality. One useful variation that is neutral under most circumstances can become the savior of a species when conditions change. Humanity has been nearly wiped out after environmental perturbations in the past. The rise of a new disease, such as smallpox, provides but one example.[4]

Smallpox is believed to have come into existence around 10,000 BC. It likely began the fall of the Roman Empire, causing the plague of Antonine in AD 160, which accounted for the deaths of almost seven million people. It was introduced to Europe around the sixth century and ravaged the continent during the Middle Ages. Western civilization can be thought of not only as the flourishing of culture, but instead as what was left over after infectious diseases decimated the population.[5]

Thanks to variation, and sometimes through sheer luck, not everyone dies in an epidemic. That's because of differences between how one person's body works versus another's. In the first wave of an epidemic, death is the rule, survival the exception; but when only the resistant survive, the resistant forms of genes rapidly increase in a population.

Genetically, the rise of one allele in particular is making news now. Called CCR5 Δ32, the genetic variant honed by smallpox is frequent in today's European populations because it is a ghost of smallpox epidemics past. Because it also provides some resistance to HIV, the mutation still piques scientific interest.[6]

But smallpox was not eradicated by physiological resistance in the form of one gene mutation. Indeed, it was something greater: a variation in behavior—the rise of new thought. Edward Jenner's mind—one that was particularly unique during the 1790s—pushed him to attempt to control an infectious disease through vaccination. Jenner's pursuits were indeed "out of the box," with strange notions that would have been considered magic to many, and indeed, his ideas were feared by some. What if his experiments were labeled as witchcraft and he had been drummed out of society for his ideas? Where would we be now? It wasn't the immune system by itself that eradicated smallpox by 1980, but an initial idea and understanding, and then an extraordinary level of persistence and cooperation—and openness to a new idea. It was exploratory behavior to learn about pathogens. It was aggressive questions and testing. Scientists and the public acted in certain ways, taking the pain of a small injection to prevent the pain of large-scale death. It took tolerance for a wide variety of ideas, and then, when a good one came along, it took more than acknowledgment of the idea. It required individuals to unselfishly abjure their own notions and individuality and accept the ideas of another.

———

If genes are selfish, why have complicated organisms such as humans and other animals evolved? Why aren't the oceans of earth just filled with a soup of countless individual self-replicating strings of DNA? Dawkins's reasoning is impeccable: genes are the fundamental unit of heredity with a single purpose, to replicate themselves.[7] It makes one think that life should not have progressed past the most simple of chemical reactions that duplicate a compound. But it did. Why?

Cooperation.

Genes may be the heritable unit, but a lonely gene in a primordial soup has no variation and a very narrow tolerance of environmental conditions. Life survives and grows by embracing cooperation. Genes cooperate to create proteins, which create cells, which specialize to create an organ, which work together to compose a body, an individual. Individuals then associate with others to form a mating pair, a society, a tribe, a population. The ability to cooperate—even as an individual—is built within our biology at the most fundamental level. Any one of our basic body cells is not as solo as it appears to be: even a single cell is actually a team.

The "powerhouse of the cell," mitochondria, provide the most fascinating example of the importance of cooperation. Within our cells are organelles, different types of little structures that function something like organs for a cell. The organelles known as mitochondria produce adenosine triphosphate, ATP. That substance is the biological gasoline that our cells use to power the chemical reactions that keep them functioning. Mitochondria are even more wondrous and unique because they are not built by our cells. Instead, they reproduce on their own, splitting like bacteria.

If they exist and reproduce within all eukaryotic cells (the cells that form the bodies of higher organisms, with true nuclei and organelles contained within membranes), where did the first mitochondrion come from? The prevailing theory is one of endosymbiosis (from the Greek for *endo* meaning "within" and *symbiosis* meaning "living together"). About 1.5 billion years ago, a progenitor of our own cells and the progenitor of the mitochondrion fused. Perhaps an amoeba-like organism ate a bacterium but didn't digest it. The bacterium found itself in a protected environment where it was provided nutrients by its host cell. In turn, the nascent mitochondrion produced chemical compounds the host couldn't make, and that in turn led to a stronger host, which directly benefited the mitochondrion.

The phenomenon of meiosis, how our body cells halve themselves to create gametes, egg and sperm, provides further evidence of mitochondria being aliens within us. Because mitochondria reproduce themselves and because sperm have no mitochondria, your mitochondria are completely matriarchal, passed solely from mother to daughter all the way back to Eve.

The meaning of this is profound: we are individuals, but even at the cellular scale, we are the product of cooperation. Two bags of genes, mitochondrial and nuclear, if unilaterally and entirely selfish, would compete with each other in a rush toward the scrap heap of evolution. Greater than the selfish gene is the miracle that it benefits genes to cooperate from the cellular to the organismal level and every step in between. Your individual body is a product of cooperation as your stomach feeds your brain and your brain finds food for your stomach. Extending the logic to individuals forming a superorganism—a cooperative society, or population, or species—each scale of life depends upon the uniqueness of the individuals within it to be able to address the next environmental challenge while simultaneously benefiting from mutualistic cooperation.

It is the great battle inherent to life: to balance between the selfish individual, who needs to be different, and the group, which demands uniformity for cooperation. This tension between the individual and the group is the fundamental tension of life.

The Borg, a scary creation within the Star Trek universe, is a collective, a hive of a species that swarms through the galaxy and assimilates other races, stomping out individuality. It is a terrifying concept: you are injected with a nano-technology that transforms you into a selfless drone and zombie, a shell with no personal thought, only the incessant ramblings of a collective mind. The Borg is the greatest threat to humans of the Star Trek future. And the biggest threat isn't even that they kill humans; it's that they rob humans of their individual personality. The reason the Borg is so powerful is that they are the perfect collective. By all being identically controlled and connected, there is no friction. Unified by one queen, they are the utmost fascist efficiency. Does the collective have more benefits than the push toward individual variation? Is there a Borg equivalent on earth?

Jamie Strange, attracted to honey, learned about beekeeping during his studies for his master's degree, but was stung more by heavy mathematics when he pursued his PhD in bee population genetics from Washington State University. His latest effort, based at the United States Department of Agriculture's bee lab in Logan, Utah, is to answer questions about the decline of bee populations in North America. He has a round, happy face, a smile framed by a goatee, and a body like a huggable bear.[8] He clearly enjoys his work, but he laments the curse of a successful scientist is relying on graduate students to do the fun stuff. They travel to all the far-flung ends of the country. "I spend more time planning other people's trips than going on my own," he says.

We tour his lab, a square box tucked away like a strip mall among experimental agricultural fields, and he leads me into a walk-in refrigerator with stacks of drinking straw-like tubes in wooden boxes. Strange pulls out a box and explains that is how that species survives the winter. He shows me an X-ray that reveals several plugs in the seven-inch tubes. Each plug is a tiny, tubular hibernaculum where the bees hole up like bears to sleep away the winter. He pulls down another box and slides it open. "This is the queen overwintering."

Another container is filled with what looks like deer feces. "These are blue orchard bees. They overwinter in cocoons." I ask about bees spinning silk, thinking it is just a spider and caterpillar thing. He says, "The silk isn't like the quality of silkworms, but they spin it from silk glands in their mandible stems. A lot of bees spin silk. It's not even that rare." He adds, with a smile, "There is one species that even spins polyester." Bees suddenly become way cooler to me.

I learn, as I tour the lab with him, that bees also excrete wax from their abdomens and create colonies that have such an advanced social structure (eusocial) that they essentially act like superorganisms— some bees like gonads, producing offspring, and others like white blood cells, cleaning the colony. It becomes clearer to me why people like Strange dedicate their lives to studying the little barbed insects.

Strange explains the many differences between honey bees and bumble bees too. I had never given it much consideration, but their differences have profound ecological and economic importance. As it turns out, it is nearly impossible to talk about bees without getting to crops and the economic importance bees have for pollinating them. The type of crop one has determines which bee is the best for pollinating, for example. Honey bees prefer plants with more pollen and avoid solanaceous plants—plants of the family Solanaceae, which includes potatoes, tomatoes, peppers, and eggplants. Honey bees tend to avoid tomatoes, because there isn't as much nectar in the flower and the pollen adheres to the flower, which requires a little vibration to shake it off—called buzz pollination.

Honey bees are bad solanaceous plant pollinators, especially in greenhouses, because they like to forage far and wide. Strange points out how important bee behavior is. "Honey bees like to move up in the air, and in greenhouses, they just fly up to the top and try to get out." Not so good for pollinating indoor plants. Honey bees don't buzz pollinate like bumble bees do, so even though both types of bee eat pollen, they do it differently. Tomatoes, and the Western culinary arts, would be nothing without bumble bees.

Another behavioral difference, and a crucial one, is how honey bees and bumble bees overwinter. Only honey bees do the famous dance within a hive, directing, through a series of shakes and body orientations, where good foraging sites are. The bees talk with each other to maximize the hive's collection efforts. Honey bee hives collect and store all that honey so they can feed their whole colony during winter, which means they need to store lots of food. They are what we typically visualize when we think of bees: Winnie the Pooh and a large perennial hive full of bees and honey.

Bumble bees avoid much of the honey bee mania. Bumble bees don't create huge, honey-laden hives. Instead, they store very little honey, and most of the queen's offspring don't survive the winter. The queens themselves go dormant, waiting to create a new hive in the spring. In the lab, Strange and I stop to look at queens in an incubator, each in its own little plastic box. They were feeding on a ball of pollen that Strange and his students had stolen from a hive somewhere and that they were using to raise hundreds of queens in the lab. A little white ball sits on the yellow ball. "That is the queen's first batch of eggs." She has to raise the first batch, and after that the young grow up and help raise successive hatchlings. New bees raise more, until they've created a huge colony of related individuals. Really related individuals.

For most animals that humans think about—that is, other humans or charismatic mammals—the offspring are a half and half mix of a male father and female mother. The gametes we produce, sperm or egg, each contain half of the blueprint for the whole organism, and two of the chromosomes in particular determine whether a child will become male or female. When females, XX, divide their cells to create egg cells, the eggs will have one X chromosome. The father, XY, will create sperm with either an X or a Y. Two XX and the zygote becomes a female, one X and one Y, and it becomes a male.

Bees work differently in their sexual events and outcomes. Potential queens disperse into the air where they join mating clouds. There, males and females vie to transfer or obtain the genetic material needed to produce the next generation. Bumble bee queens usually mate only once, but honey bees have an on-the-wing aerial orgy. During that mating extravaganza, honey bee females may store sperm from many different fathers to be used much later.

When nesting, a queen will produce eggs using the sperm she saved from her wild youth. She can, however, choose whether or not to fertilize her egg cells. If she uses stored sperm to fertilize the egg that she lays, the new bee will have the genes of both mother and father; and being *diploid*, the offspring will be female. Female bees have a passed-down set of genes from both mother and father, making them like you and me. The preponderance of females become workers. A queen can also choose to not fertilize an egg she lays. The resulting *haploid* bee has only her genes. Haploid bees become males. Think of it as a human becomes a male if he has only one X chromosome, and not two (XX are females). A male bee is equivalent.

Studying the relationships of bee genetics is mind blowing. A queen's sons are 100 percent related to her, their complete set of DNA being all hers. But because she is diploid and they are haploid, she is only 50 percent related to her sons. The workers, however, share 100 percent of their father's DNA (he is haploid and passes on 100 percent of his genes) but have only 50 percent of their mother's DNA (she is diploid but passes on half of her genes into her eggs), so the daughters are 75 percent related to each other. The math is somewhat confusing, but the crucial aspect to remember if comparing bees and humans, is that the sister bees share many more copies of the same genes than human siblings. Mostly.

Bees, being more variable within a hive than once thought, have other tricks to increase the variation within their hive. For example, many sisters are only half-sisters because the queen typically mates with different males but stores all their sperm. The queen, by mating with many males, can create subfamilies. Colonies within colonies. "Subfamilies provide a buffer and resilience," Strange explains. They ensure genetic variability, even within a bee colony, long thought to be a singular superorganism.

Strange, still a beekeeper himself, continues, "Beekeepers know that each colony has a different personality." In the simplest observation, "some are docile," he says. I suspect that if researchers investigated the notion, they'd find that different hives fall differently into brave or timid or aggressive continuums like the animals discussed so far.

Humans rely on and closely cooperate with bees: they feed us by pollinating the crops that we feed them with. Due to bees' economic importance, most recent research has focused on things that can kill a hive. "Some hives," Strange says, "are disease resistant." They do not resist the disease by having internal antibodies or improved physiologies. Rather, they do it using behavioral tendencies: personalities within an almost genetically identical hive.

Take *Varroa destructor*, for example. With a name like that, it has to be something of a problem, and indeed, it is contributing to the concern about loss of bees from colony collapse disorder. *V. destructor* is a pesky mite that stows away on foraging worker bees. The mites feed on the hemolymph (the insect equivalent of blood) of adults, but when they get into a hive, the mites find their way to the larva just before the brood cell is sealed shut so that the larvae can develop.[9] That is where the mayhem begins. The "foundress" female mite will lay five or six eggs on the pupa while she feeds on it herself. Her first egg, unfertilized, becomes a male, as would an unfertilized bee egg. All the rest of her brood will be females. When the eggs hatch, they all join in to feed on the developing pupa too.

Males and females mate and then leave the cell when their very weak host emerges from its cell. The female mites then attach to another adult bee or invade another incubation cell to feast and reproduce on another pupa. The infection grows exponentially, weakening and killing bee larvae as the mites reproduce. Most bee colonies will be dead within a year or two if the mites are left unchecked.

But some bees have developed a way to counteract an infection. Workers within some colonies patrol outside brooding chambers. They somehow have the ability to detect when a pupa is infected with the mite, and if they find one, the bee pulls out the doomed larva and mites and kills them all. One sister is lost, but the sanitizing bees stop the growth of the mite infection. "It is an individual behavioral trait within a colony," Strange points out, "that beekeepers can select for" to create new mite-resistant colonies.

Due to their incredible degree of social cooperation, fascinating genetics, and multiple scales of personality and behavior, science can learn a lot from bees. For all the talk about genetic relatedness within a hive, bees are not the Borg. Infertile workers cooperate by feeding their queens, and in exchange, the queens pass on some of the sister workers' selfish genes. Bees, even those of different species, may gain by cooperating.

Among Strange's vast array of publications, one paper caught my eye. It describes how Strange collected different female bumble bees in the spring and brought them back to the lab to create new colonies.[10] There, he housed them in plush nest boxes in one of three arrangements: alone, paired with another queen of the same species, or paired with two honey bee workers. Solitary females were rarely successful at starting a new colony. Those with the honey bee helpers were almost twice as successful. Putting two queens together—who could be the most competitive but also are most aligned for cooperation—did by far the best, almost four times better than the solitary females. It's not that individuals don't cooperate more in nature but rather that researchers tend to focus on the conflicts instead. If scientists and beekeepers alike can delve into the variation of bees, and identify more surprising ways that the animals can work together or investigate the variety of "personalities" of hives and their subfamilies, the results could be as significant as finding the secrets to controlling colony collapse disorder.

———

James Surowiecki begins his argument in the *Wisdom of the Crowds*, by recounting a famous exercise by Francis Galton, who, in 1906 in Plymouth, England, attended a livestock exhibition.[11] A well-to-do and famous statistician, Galton toiled to demonstrate that the hoi polloi were of inferior stock and mental acuity. His ideas were that the diversity of the crowd was a weakness, and that political power must be held by the well bred.

To test the masses, he arranged for 787 people, none of whom had any particular specialty or experience with livestock, to guess the dressed weight of an ox. They looked at the animal and then wrote down their guess of what the living, breathing ox would weigh after it had been slaughtered and cleaned. He made the direct assertion that the average person would be as stupid about choosing a political candidate as they would be off the mark when they guessed the weight of the ox.

In the story, Galton collects the guesses from all the people, expecting a few more knowledgeable or lucky people to make a guess close to the actual weight, but he expected that most people, with a lack of training, would be bone-headedly wrong. The actual weight of the dressed ox was 1,198 pounds. The average of the crowd's guess was 1,197 pounds. The collective guess was off by less than one-tenth of a percent. Essentially perfect.

The experiment, and indeed the rest of Surowiecki's book, is an ironic lesson in the diversity of individuals in groups. There are certain threats to diversity in modern society, such as elites disdaining others but also the rank and file rejecting those not like them. The lesson of *Wisdom of the Crowds* isn't in which group is better than another but in the observation that widely variable individuals, when formed into a collective, can create a group that is wiser than its individuals. It should remind us that we could eugenically produce breeds of smart people trained in a specific task, such as guessing the weight of a bull. Is it wise for all people to have the same knowledge, skills, and abilities? Relying on only one elite class? The greater significance of Surowiecki's point is that diversity may feel inefficient, but when individuals work within a collective they can actually accomplish tasks better than if they were to go it alone—even with all the conflicting styles and opinions.

The balanced cooperation of diverse individuals has become the strength of life: mutualism, interactions within and between species that are beneficial to both, be it plebeian, bee, or tomato. Scientists tend to focus on strife more than cooperation, but we ought to keep focus on the idea of mutualism, because there would not be the diversity of personalities all throughout the animal world if individuals didn't find ways to cooperate.

What if individuals couldn't cooperate? The worst case scenario does sometimes occur. Consider the example of an individual who is focused only on his own resource acquisition. He'll exploit others without any regard for their needs. Without checks, those that act that way would acquire more resources by outcompeting the gracious and cooperative others. In the short term, of course, such disregard could lead to conflict and strife, but in the longer term, the effects can be catastrophic. These self-centered individuals, hogging resources, would reproduce more. Their progeny would replicate selfishly too—such that neither cooperative nor self-limiting individuals would quickly dominate the population. Such self-indulgence leads to the struggling and mass suffering of others, as the unilaterally rapacious individuals destroy their society from within.

In a moral framework, this disregard for any cooperation is what I consider evil. In a biological framework, the concept is equivalently atrocious, an attack on the nature of life itself, and it occurs in nature too. Not only between us but also within us. What would such a complete, unbalanced aggressiveness be called? In our bodies, it is called *cancer*. Cancer is the effect of cells reproducing completely unrestrained, at the cost of other cells in the body. Cancerous cells dominate the food supply and poison their surroundings. They divide without end until the strength of their dominating individuality kills their environment, the collective, and dooms their own existence. Societies can have cancers too, when individual sociopaths reject the value of others different from themselves. Individuality, then, is an essential element for successful life, but it does have a limit: when it is not balanced with the benefits of cooperation.

Behavioral variation—which is exactly the phenomenon that results in a wide variety of personalities—creates a collective strength. Whether it is bold discoverers of cures for smallpox, brave creators of flying machines, or cautious lovers caring for others, the diversity allows populations to adapt to the threats of environmental change. The mechanism for reducing diversity could be through speciesism, genocide, or eugenics—they are the same thing. They all favor an ideal, using a subsample of traits, over variation; as moral biology, they are wrong.

How do we balance the needs of the many with the needs of the few? The adaptive benefits of emotion and individuality were not lost on Darwin, who argued in *The Expression of the Emotions in Man and Animals* that feelings developed as fertilizer for sociality. He understood that animals have feelings too, and they need their own signals and moralities to work together as individuals. Morality, for humans and animals, is a game of optimization: the selfish herd, the generous gene, and creating the greatest good by simultaneously collaborating and incorporating our differences. How, and by what rules, humans and animals establish our cooperative groups—or not—is the source of our strength and the root of our atrocities. One biological definition of morality is the optimization of individual cooperation intraspecifically and interspecifically.[12] We have to be ourselves, but we also have to play well with other humans and other animals.

CHAPTER 9

Pairing Singularities

Chance was a "big bundle of loving . . . he was cuddly," said Sandra Fisher when she described her Brahman bull, Chance, on the radio program *This American Life*.[1] Neither Sandra nor her husband, Ralph, had seen a bull so docile before. Chance readily let children crawl all over him. White, long-horned, and passive, he became famous for his temperament, which allowed him to appear in movies and on late night shows. Chance died too young, which broke the heart of his owners.

After reading that animals were being cloned at Texas A&M, an hour and a half from their house, Sandra and Ralph convinced researchers to clone Chance. Pulling DNA from a preserved biopsy of Chance's, the scientists reincarnated Chance ten months after he died. Second Chance was born, and the Fishers concluded he was identical in appearance to their previous bull. There were many behavioral similarities too. The clone and original both raised their head and closed their eyes when they ate, different from other bulls. They both chose the same place to lay to rest. "We got him back!" the Fishers declared when they brought Second Chance home.

The scientists were skeptical, but believing in a direct reincarnation was harmless—at first. Second Chance looked the same as the original, and the Fishers focused on the similarities. But as he grew, Second Chance's temperament began to differ from Chance's. After the bull's first birthday party, Second Chance attacked Ralph while being led back to his stall. Chance dislocated Ralph's shoulder, and the young bull's horns nearly killed him. Then on another occasion, the clone of the gentlest bull on earth threw Ralph into the air and gored him. Ralph landed in the hospital with eighty new stitches and a hairline fracture in his spine. The Fishers were forced to acknowledge that Second Chance, a clone of the first, looked like an identical twin, but the personality of the bull was definitely different.

The story is not unique in the sense that people often bond so strongly with their pets that they are desperate to bring them back. Geneticists are deluged with requests to recreate family pets. But genes don't work that way. Individual animals cannot be replicated any more than identical twins can be considered the same person. Genes are not perfect in their replication and are strongly influenced by the environment through epigenetic effects. Even clones are not more alike than identical twins. If you have a favorite pet or animal you love, the time you spend in your bond now is all you will ever have. There will never be another. Every individual is as unique and impermanent as a snowflake.

Bonds can form between two humans or between a human and a pet, a wild animal, or livestock. What is real is that humans and animals form bonds as individuals, with other individuals.[2] Bonding is how individuals overcome the tension between desperately needing to express our own personality with the equally intense need to cooperate with a collective. How do two very different animals, with different life strategies, figure out how to live together? What are the mechanisms animals use to cooperate?

Spider monkeys (*Ateles geoffroyi*) form protean groups, sometimes splitting up to go their own ways and other times rejoining to interact socially. Rejoining can be a dangerous time: a pecking order has to be reestablished. The social friction can be resolved through bickering and fighting, but it can also be resolved in other ways.

Filippo Aureli and Colleen Schaffner watched the social circus of a group of spider monkeys and monitored how well individuals interacted after new groups formed.[3] The researchers observed fifteen individuals that engaged in hugs when they were reunited with their fellow monkeys. That subgroup did not display or receive any aggressive behavior after embracing. When monkeys didn't embrace, however, disharmony and disagreements erupted. When joining a group without first embracing, the mean hourly postfusion aggression rate was 0.56, or about a fight every other hour. The authors concluded that developing rituals is a way to bypass more violent means of establishing pecking orders. They noted that humans can learn much by watching how other animals navigate interpersonal relationships: "As human societies are also characterized by frequent fissions and fusions, our results suggest that research on the potential function of such greetings in reducing tension and facilitating tolerance at reunions may contribute to the understanding of human conflict management."[4]

Spider monkeys reconnect peacefully by hugging. When groups of monkeys reconnect, they embrace. Arms so employed, it forces two animals to be close, and in a way that they are not hitting each other. The tension deescalates.

Bonobos are another species particularly famous for rectifying their conflicts peacefully, especially through touching and even sexual activity.[5] Females, as a form of peacemaking and bonding, will engage in genito-genital rubbing, where one female clings to another like an infant, and they press their crotches together and frantically rub sideways against each other. The rituals of bonobos, including their make love not war strategy, creates bonds that hold their social groups together.

We've examined the use of rituals before, such as the silk-ball gift giving that fly males use to seduce females (chapter 2), as a means of promoting harmony between individuals. Rituals are behavioral norms used to decrease tension and increase unity between different individuals. Humans shake hands and embrace like spider monkeys. Couples kiss and make up with sexual activity after fights, like bonobos. Humans unify when they sing pop anthems together or form spiritual connections while sharing religious rituals.

I have fond memories of growing up Catholic, especially of the Christmas Mass. Candles were everywhere. Beautiful decorations and garlands draped through the already ornate church. Incense wafting over stained glass and statuary. The words of the Mass were standard, familiar readings from the Bible every year, but there was magic and wonder in the familiarity of the repetition. Everyone in that church, whether tall or short, big or small, old or young, in that dreamy land of a perfect Mass, was my closest friend. We, all different, were all one.

Humans and animals alike create rituals, which promote cooperation at the times when we most need it. In humans and undoubtedly other animals, the rituals, however, are still only an outward display. Rituals unify by creating a common and clearly interpretable mode of communication, but they are external, a necessary tool needed to soften the edges between different personalities. Rituals are stereotypic practices that individuals use to align their behaviors and individual tendencies. But the rituals are only those things we see; something more grows within us to help us resist the half of natural selection that demands competition.

Lynne Gilbert-Norton works with Canines with a Cause, matching a particular person with a particular dog.[6] She roams the dog shelters in and around Salt Lake City to search for dogs with personalities suitable for their eventual task of inspiring confidence and stability in a troubled veteran. It takes the right dog with the right balance of predator and prey drives. Not all dogs can do it; they have to be brave, bold, and confident enough to explore with their companion, but homebody and social enough to be comfortable and calm when nothing needs to happen. The dog's job is to form emotional bonds between individuals of very different species, creating trust, understanding, and ultimately healing.

The Canines with a Cause program prides itself in "saving three lives."[7] First, there is the dog Gilbert-Norton finds in a shelter. Second, there are the initial trainers, with lives as tragic as the incarcerated dogs. Gilbert-Norton visits a prison to find inmates who are capable and willing to teach the dogs basic obedience and commands. Canines with a Cause found that the transition is good for the dog and the inmate. It lessens the burden of training on the third life saved, a veteran with the psychological scars of war.

At the women's prison, Gilbert-Norton shares, the prisoners "have been through everything possible." It's a tremendous opportunity for them to obtain educational and coping skills as they learn about their dog's behavior—which undeniably leads to a better understanding of how they communicate with, or try to control, others. They learn how to alter and improve behaviors—both their dog's and their own—as they bond with their dog.

The program is not easy, however, and the women are from tough backgrounds. Many of them have been incarcerated for murder. They've grown up in tragic or horrendous situations. They have tremendous personal challenges. It's a transition for them, as the dog they receive may be the "first living thing they have been allowed to honestly interact with. No one else in the prison trusts them."

From the dogs, the inmates learn about trust and love. They learn how to build a relationship and about the effects of positive reinforcement. Everything they learn in the justice system, Gilbert-Norton notes, is punishment. How do you return to society when the only tool you know when interacting with others is to cause them pain? By being dog trainers, the inmates can learn something about how to forge new relationships and how to improve their own interactions with other people. There's "a lot of drama in a women's prison. One lady used to get into infractions all the time." Then, she learned how to work with dogs, and "now she has become the mediator" at the prison, Gilbert-Norton proudly notes. The women, by bonding with a particular dog, learn the benefits of cooperation.

After the dogs finish their initial training at the prison, they are ready for the veterans. "The army," Gilbert-Norton says, has a "dominance-based approach to life too." They learn to problem solve and communicate in a very different way from civilians. Amid the uncertain violence of modern war, with plain-clothed combatants and improvised explosive devices, it is sometimes too much to expect a smooth transition between combat and civilian life. A soldier may need a constant buddy, like the camaraderie that forms in foxholes, to help navigate a path through post-traumatic stress disorder. A veteran may desire and teach a dog to walk ahead, giving an uneasy person a little extra space. Or the dog can trail behind, literally having the veteran's back. Dogs can wake a troubled soldier up from a nightmare. A trained dog is not the only product, however, as the process forces the veterans to learn additional tools of trust and communication. They learn to bond.

"It isn't like they get the dog and it fixes them," Gilbert-Norton clarifies. The process of coming to training and having the dog with them is the thing. It can help them with the symptoms. It can help them reincorporate into a less dangerous society. Having a particular animal to bond with may seem miraculous, but it's work, not a miracle.

When we talk about a bond between two individuals, we often talk of "chemistry." But as much as we try to create algorithms for relationships, there is more to them than filling a checklist of ideal attributes. One can go to online dating services and enter all the right qualities. I've certainly done that in my dating, listing out how far away she'd live from me, that she *has* to love animals and the outdoors, skiing, whitewater kayaking, reading, and adventure. In truth, I've met perfect women who have had all the right qualifications on paper, but in spending time together, our relationships felt vapid and flat. Fortunately or unfortunately, love is not a checklist. It is about matching unique, but complementary, personalities.

There is something powerful and ineffable about a connection between two individuals (two people as lovers or friends, or a man and his cat, as the case may be). Humans and animals form bonds innately, instinctually. We may not be aware of it, or know exactly how it works, but we know it when we feel it. And recently scientists have begun to measure the effects personality, preference, and the formation of bonds.

My favorite research on the topic is Bernhard Fink and his colleagues' paper "Men's Personality and Women's Perception of Their Dance Quality."[8] The researchers, based out of the University of Göttingen, Germany, and Northumbria University in the United Kingdom, signed up a sample of forty-eight heterosexual men between eighteen and forty-two years old. None of the men were professional dancers, but more or less normal guys in good health. The researchers used a version of the NEO PI test (as we saw in chapter

2) to generate personality scores, with metrics for neuroticism, extroversion, openness, conscientiousness, and agreeableness.

In the study, Fink played a basic drum beat and took video recordings of the men dancing. Then, to control for other affects, such as the looks or stature or bodily proportions, the scientists used computer software to create a standardized male avatar that performed the same movements as each man. Then they played the dancing avatars for fifty-three women from seventeen to fifty-seven years old and asked the women to rate each man from one for an extremely bad dancer to seven for an extremely good dancer.

The results were pretty clear. Most women, given the stripped-down, soundless, and soulless figures on the computer screen, were not overly impressed with the dancing. They ranked the men from 1.8 to 4.7 on the one to seven dance scale. Tough judges.

But that was only the baseline for the study. The researchers did something unique, in that they then correlated the men's measured personalities to the women's scoring of the avatar. Correlating personality scores with dance ratings, the researchers found that women favored men with certain personality traits that they somehow detected in the featureless avatars.

Specifically, women classified men who were conscientious and agreeable as good dancers. Extroversion was also correlated positively with dance quality. The correlation was weak between dance quality and neuroticism, but it was negative. That is, the more jealous and resentful of others a man was (neuroticism), the more negative were the women's judgments of his dance quality. Thus, as individuals struggle to find and cooperate with their mates, the interplay between physiology and behavior is subliminal. There is more to bonding than what is readily apparent. Were the women rating men as good dancers because the dancing in itself was attractive, or were they able to use the dance moves to help assess favorable personality traits too?

The study suggests that physiology and movements, complex behaviors such as dancing, are related to an expression of personality. And women somehow pick up on that. Remember, men, that when you are on the dance floor and hoping to waltz with that special someone, women are not only judging you for the physicality of your dancing but are intuiting about your personality too. Your moves communicate whether the chemistry could be right and lead to more than one dance.

———

Elizabeth Liverman's Equisyn horses range from being social and outgoing to more introverted and focused on getting a job done. Another aspect is closely intertwined with the work of Equisyn, however, and that is the intense relationship—a bond—that develops between a horse and a client, or between Liverman and her horses.

This examination of individual personality would fall short if we didn't investigate how differences in individuals create emergent properties within groups. Groups are cemented together with bonds between individuals, and as different as horses are from people, the emotional connection between a particular horse and a particular person can be incredibly strong. Out of the dozens of horses that Liverman knows well, I ask for an example of one that stands out from all the rest.

"I can give you two," she says.

"The first time that I saw Teak, he came out of the field and came to me at the fence. The owner told me that he never does that, but I knew right then that I had to have that horse." It was as if she was describing love at first sight. Some of us have met a person for the first time and immediately felt a strange euphoria of emotional connection, butterflies in the stomach, the chemistry of an immediate bond. Liverman was describing a similar event with Teak, but she refined her notion: "That horse chose me."

Teak was Liverman's friend and guardian right from the start. "I'd use him as my boyfriend judge. If Teak did not like the guy, I dropped him." It was a high bar, because Teak rarely liked anyone else besides Liverman. "It turns out he liked Dave, so I married him."

They called Teak Dr. Jekyll and Mr. Hyde at the stable. When Liverman was there he was happy, but when she was gone, he'd pin his ears back and kick, become mischievous. His Dr. Jekyll side came out in her absence. Teak learned how to slide the bolt back on his stall gate. He'd not immediately run off, however, but the wily Thoroughbred would instead systematically fiddle with and release the horses from the adjacent stalls. Teak was special; he affected Liverman's life to the point of helping her choose a husband, but she says he wasn't the most important horse to her. That was definitely Rennie.

Liverman acquired the big Clydesdale-Thoroughbred cross when the mare was two years old. Rennie was standoffish and did not like to interact with people: INFJ. Liverman tried to track down the horse's history, attempting to figure out why she was so shy. She bought her from a dealer who said he found her at an auction, but when Liverman looked into auction records, she couldn't find the history. She figured that Rennie had been sort of a foster child, a horse that was moved from person to person. That would explain her being so guarded. "I suspected that she was stolen."

"Rennie was not at all trusting." Liverman spent lot of time just being with Rennie, not necessarily riding even, just being present. "Within a few weeks, she started to change. As we worked together it was totally obvious that we had bonded." The horse would follow Liverman everywhere as she went about her chores. Physically, Rennie would stay close, but if she couldn't, she'd track her companion with her eyes and ears.

When riding, Rennie seemed to know what Liverman was thinking before she thought it. On one occasion Liverman was getting frustrated trying to figure out what she was doing wrong when guiding Rennie over a series of jumps called cavalettis. It just wasn't working. But then "It was like I heard it in my head to adjust the cavalettis and to sit back more." The thought wasn't a reasoned one. Liverman describes the connection between her and her horse as if it was some sort of Vulcan mind meld. The voice she heard felt external. She could process information in a way that she would not have been able to without the bond with that particular horse. She followed the inner voice, and they cleared the jumps perfectly after that.

Then she describes another time that demonstrated the intense emotional bond between Rennie and her. During the Great Recession, her husband had lost his company and his job. Her house and horses were in jeopardy. It looked as though they would lose everything. Liverman was raking the stalls when she became overwhelmed and broke down crying. Rennie, who had her face in her feed bucket, stopped. She ignored her food and walked to Liverman and lowered her neck and jaw, cuddling her into her body. She calmed Liverman down and breathed slowly and calmly into her ears. As she tells me this story, her eyes well up.

"When I stopped crying, she actually licked the tears," she says. Horses don't do that.

That was a bond between those two *individuals*.

I explain the purpose of my research to Liverman and tell her of the distain for anthropomorphism that scientists have had. That just because we humans feel something, it does not mean another animal will feel it. I ask her what she thinks of this.

"I think that's bullshit," she says without hesitating. "It is a way that mankind tries to show superiority." She may have a point. We certainly have egotistical baggage and most certainly strive to distance ourselves from the other animals. Liverman, however, acknowledges one way that animals are indeed different: "Animals are honest."

She asserts that there are still many mysteries about animals, that there are more aspects of animal communication that we have not detected yet. I recall David Stoner saying the same thing regarding cougars, that we are mostly in the dark about understanding them and their behaviors.

Liverman points out an irony in human hubris too. "Animals give us these things unconditionally. Look at the science behind it now." And she's right, as modern authors are increasingly investigating the emotional intelligence of individual animals.[9] There is a mainstreaming of something many of us already knew intuitively. "Most of us have had a time when we didn't feel well and had a cat or dog or another companion that provided comfort." Humans and animals form strong, emotional, and mutualistic bonds.

"I completely trust my horses," she says, and it reminds me of how Lori Schmidt described the particular wolves she bonded with. The relationship, the bond, is summed up with a simple concept: trust.

———

Bonds between individuals can have many forms, the concept of biophilia, for example, which Edward O. Wilson defines as our "innate tendency to focus on life and lifelike processes."[10] He argues that within each person is an innate love and attraction to nature. We value novelty and diversity through both instinct and reason. We are primed from birth to have encounters with particular wild or domestic animals that can be intensely emotional and long-lasting. Like Wilson, many other scientists aren't immune to forming bonds with their subjects either. Recall the wolves described by researchers in chapter 1. Each scientist had a unique story about a particular individual. More than just amusing anecdotes, they demonstrate the unique connections scientists can form with their animal subjects.

David Stoner, the cougar-studying postdoc, talks about a particular mountain lion he worked with that was like no other. "There was a female . . . Number 6." His eyes sparkle when he recounts the story, almost like a proud father talking about the accomplishments of his young daughter. "And Number 6's sister was 68, which is the year that I was born."[11]

Stoner caught Number 6 on two particularly memorable occasions. The first time she was captured, they had chased her all day. She would not pause to cower in a tree. By the time they finally cornered her, it was nighttime. They were trudging through deep high-mountain snows. "It was cold as hell, and I was a neophyte," he says. Darting wildlife seems so easy on TV. The pursuers shoot, the animal passes out. But in reality, there are so many other factors. In the winter, ketamine can freeze in the syringes before the darts are shot. The needle clogs, and the darted animal may receive a partial dose, or none at all.

"She wouldn't go down." Stoner frets. "I just kept giving her bigger dosages." He knows that ketamine has a priceless advantage of a wide margin for error and safety, and that overdoses are rare. After several shots, he finally got her sleeping and lowered her from the tree. "I had her on my lap, kept her warm and comforted her as I would a pet housecat," as her body fought the drug. An hour later, when he felt she was recovering well, they affixed the radio collar, put her in a safe place, and left to hike out in the middle of the night. He went to check on her the next day and was happy to find that she was fine.

Stoner learned her habits by following her movements and studying where she went and what she did. When the battery in her collar was going dead, they had to find, capture, and recollar her. Stoner already felt that there was something unique about the lion who had come to be known as "Ketamine Queen," but the bond between them strengthened during their second encounter.

The second time he captured her, it required another daylong chase. That time, rather than climbing up a tree, she ran into a large sort of drainpipe that led into an old mining building. Inside the structure the conduit led into a large underground space, like a basement or a cistern. Stoner walked on loose and precarious planks above the cornered cougar. He removed a few boards and peered down into the space below. Number 6 was sitting on a concrete dividing wall. Startled, she jumped off the wall and onto the floor. It was, unfortunately, full of water, with a thin sheet of ice over the top. Number 6 broke through and was left wading.

He was horrified to hear the paddling and panting below and was relieved when she climbed up onto the sheet of ice. His adrenaline was pumping and he was desperate. He took a shot and missed. It was dark, and they were at a high angle, so a decent shot was impossible. He lost several darts into the abyss. Improvising, he found a pile of old fire hose, and Stoner wrapped it around a pipe and used it to rappel into the basement. He describes his effort, leaning off the wall against an old hose and chambering the last dart, "like a Navy SEAL," except that he was "shaking like a leaf." The ice was too thin to stand on, so he braced against the wall and aimed the pistol. He shot. It stuck. She slumped, sleeping. Stoner used her collar to drag her to him and had his companion pull them both up. He dried her, wrapped her in a blanket, and replaced her collar. "They are incredibly tough animals," he smiles—and they have at least nine lives.

Number 6 survived and produced one male and one female kitten. The female kitten stayed to live in the same area; Stoner monitored the kitten, who also became a successful mother, for ten years. The male dispersed all the way across the very populated Salt Lake Valley and took up residence around the Sundance ski area. Number 6 was a challenging animal who provided numerous data points that helped Stoner acquire his PhD, but she was also a caring and innovative mother. Stoner's favorite cat died on the mountain several years later of unknown causes. When he found her body, she had curled up "like a house cat on a bed," and it looked as if she had just gone to sleep.

Listening to him tell the story, I could sense a unique bond there, between a cougar and a man. "She taught me a lot about these animals and how adaptable they are," he says. Her home range encompassed a working mine with a lot of human activity. The textbook cougar would not have tolerated that. Number 6, however, used human-made structures to cache her prey. She'd raise her kittens in old pipes. She'd roam into neighborhoods at night to take advantage of roadkill. Stoner describes her as an "ultimately pragmatic animal." She used what was available to her advantage. She was different from all the others, never to be seen again.

A eulogy for Gretchen.

This is to say I loved that particular dog. As a scientist I can acknowledge that my feelings of love, the firing of neurons, is a capability wired into mammalian brains. Loving animals, even as the hunter that I am, is a natural component of my physiology, my biophilia. I am primed for it innately. Other mammals—and who knows the depths of emotion in other animals?—are equipped with similar physiological structures and brain regions, so they undoubtedly feel some of the same emotions that we humans do. When interacting with an animal, therefore, I do not mind imagining that the licks or nuzzles or purrs are given with the same motivation and intent with which I feel and interpret them.

The strengths of our bonds and ability to communicate between species can help us, as in the case of Canines with a Cause, but the loss of love can also devastate us. I recall when Gretchen, my search and rescue, beer-fetching companion, gradually lost control of her mind and body. It took years for her legs to stiffen and slow her, but the wearing of her frame was ineluctable. Then her eyes grew more and more opaque when her medications weren't helping anymore.

Her hearing started to fail, and I worried about the beautiful mind wasting away behind her cloudy eyes.

Gretchen still knew me with her nose, a sense that had been so honed in her that the dimming of her eyes and ears may have been a little less important. For a time, she could smell her way through the house. But moving got harder and harder for her. It wasn't that she was in obvious physical pain, but I am certain there was intense mental anguish. Especially because Gretchen was the dog that *reasoned* through challenges.

She trusted me more than any other. In her prime she had readily jumped into a canoe or off a dock with confidence—all I had to do was snap my fingers. She climbed ladders, crawled through culverts, and followed the wind to find missing people. I trusted her and her abilities beyond any other.

Then there was the day I found her stuck, staring blindly into a corner. She was moving her nose from wall to wall, left and right. She was addled, lost in her own familiar dining room. Then came the day when she awoke on the same floor, bewildered, lying in a puddle of her own urine. She sniffed it, distraught, and stared sightlessly into the distance as I cleaned her. I could not fathom how the most amazing dog that had ever walked the earth had been reduced to a helpless shell, embarrassed by her own mind and body.

A good veterinarian will tell you that when it is time to put a pet down, you know. You know when the limit has been reached. They do not give you a guide or checklist other than to say to use your heart. You know when it is time.

Gretchen rested on a pillow. She seemed so weary, troubled. I hugged her and loved her, and, trusting me completely, she took her final, relaxed breath. In a second, she was relaxed, out of anguish. I kissed and petted and wept uncontrollably. I still cry when I think of her and miss her terribly.

It wasn't the death of a dog. It wasn't the death of my pet, my companion. It was the death of Gretchen. I don't give a damn what the scientists and philosophers think. She had emotion and understanding. She had her own unique personality and potential. She and I had a unique bond, and I am not crazy for believing it or for the depth of emotion I feel about her loss. There will never be another like her again.

———

Put simply, the bond is love. Love is the positive force, the intense biochemical and emotional feedback mechanism that makes us, as individuals, want to cooperate with others, especially with *certain* others. We actually want to love for intensely selfish reasons: because it feels so overwhelmingly good. And the emotional reaction, as Darwin concluded, makes every bit of evolutionary sense.

But love is also more complex than that, driving our behaviors past moments of instant gratification. It is not only unicorns and rainbows; it will also cause discomfort in relationships between individuals. I make my son brush his teeth, eat his vegetables, and go to bed on time. Yes, in some ways I torment him with these little nags, but I create that conflict and disharmony precisely because I love him. There is that paradox in love. Truly loving someone can require annoying them. Love can lead to the pain of childbirth, as in the case of my son's mother. It can also require the pain and irony of the truest love, a willingness to completely let go and set them free, also in the case of my son's mother.

People speak of love in ways that sound trivial. We say that we *love* cats, or dogs. And we do. We bond with individuals within our species and with those of other species. We can provide an individual pleasure when we feed and care for a pet, or give the species evolutionarily "pleasure" by encouraging its genes to propagate. This all results from the programming of love.

Personality exists in all animal species, and that behavioral variation is a fundamental force that enables evolution. Scientists and laypersons alike—including politicians—ought to support the idea that *diversity* is not only a feel-good, "politically correct" word but also a scientifically demonstrable strength in populations. In the long run, variation—especially behavioral—will allow humans to survive the turmoil of nature. We should acknowledge that people need one another as individuals and find ways to soften the effects when personalities, hopes, dreams, and desires conflict. All of us would do better if we learned to accept individual personality in all animals, even when it means giving up a little of our own individuality.

The mechanism within us to soften disharmony is to form bonds and mutualisms between individuals. Written by a scientist, it sounds so dry, but it is the biological need to cooperate that eventually leads to the poetry. Will humans let go of the notion that we are superior enough not to need any other species? Will we instead turn toward optimizing our bonds and cooperation with all of them? There will be pain and suffering in the world forever, and life cannot exist without it or death, but the quality of our relationships and our existence can be optimized.

Humans can choose to acknowledge and trust one another—other humans and other animals—even if it seems grating or counter to our own values. In the first pages of this book, for example, I describe Pingüino as a loud, demanding, and annoying cat. I have learned much since then. He taught me that sometimes you need to be an asshole to survive. He's also taught me that sometimes purring is better than using claws. Now, he still presents a unique personality and strength of will that can be challenging at times, but he also has much to offer. He sits snuggled and reassuringly on my lap, and I can't deny there is also something about him that I love. He's not a pack animal, not social the way humans or dogs are, but I have no doubt that this cat considers me a good friend and feels a degree of brotherly love, as if we are in the same foxhole together. There is that bond between us. Love. The mechanism that compels two animals—with strikingly different forms and personalities—to thrive together.

Acknowledgments

First thanks go as always to my son, Fox, for his patience while I try to be the best father possible, which includes understanding and accepting his transition from being a youthful extension of his parents to becoming a great adult in his own right—with his own personality. I am so proud to be your father. The sign you pecked out as a first grader, "From fox, To dad, good typing dad!," will always hang above my desk and inspire me as I write.

The idea for this book came both from my years of observing differences between dozens of individual coyotes in the field and captivity and from the fruitful mind of Laura Wood, my champion at Fine Print Literary Management. I appreciate Laura's encouragement and insights and her generosity with editing too; her efforts were far above and beyond her required duties. Will Myers, my editor at Beacon, has been thoughtful and doggedly dedicated. His edits improved the manuscript far beyond my initial ramblings, and I can't thank him enough for the effort he repeatedly put into the text; his contagious enthusiasm and excitement for this project was particularly encouraging. Thanks to Susan Lumenello and Andrea Lee for their patience and thoroughness in correcting my errors and to all the behind-the-scene professionals at Beacon for guiding the project along.

I thank the many scientists whose work I quoted from their primary publications. For me, this book was undoubtedly the most fun to research ever. I hope the reader enjoyed learning about personality in everything from spiders to water striders to bees and crabs, and all the others, as much as I did. Extra thanks to Renée Duckworth, Elizabeth Liverman, Denise Cheung, David Stoner, Lynne

Gilbert-Norton, Patrick Myers, Lori Schmidt, and Jamie Strange for taking time to talk with me about their research and related ideas.

There are far too many friends and family to thank who were so supportive of me during the years it took to think about and then gather the material and write this book. I especially appreciate the enthusiasm of two particular little "squirrels," but most of all I thank Tara Jorgenson, who prodded me just the right amount so that I'd develop and submit the proposal, and then supported me so selflessly as I wrote.

Notes

CHAPTER 1: MY CAT AND DOGMA

1. The Wildlife Society, "Final Position Statement: Feral and Free-Ranging Domestic Cats," Wildlife Society, 2011.

2. Carl Safina, *Beyond Words: What Animals Think and Feel* (New York: New Picador, 2016).

3. Marc Bekoff and Jane Goodall, *The Emotional Lives of Animals: A Leading Scientist Explores Animal Joy, Sorrow, and Empathy—and Why They Matter* (Novato, CA: New World Library, 2008).

4. Jeffrey Moussaieff Masson and Susan McCarthy, *When Elephants Weep: The Emotional Lives of Animals* (New York: Delta, 1996); Cynthia Moss and Martyn Colbeck, *Echo of the Elephants: The Story of an Elephant Family* (New York: William Morrow, 1993); G. A. Bradshaw, *Elephants on the Edge: What Animals Teach Us About Humanity* (New Haven, CT: Yale University Press, 2009).

5. Frans de Waal, *The Bonobo and the Atheist: In Search of Humanism Among the Primates* (New York: W. W. Norton, 2014).

6. Charles Darwin, *The Expression of the Emotions in Man and Animals* (London: John Murray, 1872).

7. Ibid.

8. George John Romanes, *Animal Intelligence* (London: K. Paul, Trench, 1882).

9. C. Lloyd Morgan, *An Introduction to Comparative Psychology* (London: Charles Scribner's Sons, 1896).

10. Ibid., 120.

11. Ibid.

12. Judith Goodenough, Betty McGuire, and Robert A. Wallace, *Perspectives on Animal Behavior* (Hoboken, NJ: Wiley, 1993).

13. C. D. Fryar, Q. Gu, and C. L. Ogden, "Anthropometric Reference Data for Children and Adults: United States, 2007–2010," National Center for Health Statistics, Vital and Health Statistics Series 11, no. 252 (2012).

14. To calculate the chance of a male being average weight, I started with the weight of males in the United States from CDC data. The mean weight

(in pounds) is 195. The sample size was 5,651, and the standard error was 0.99. Using this information, the standard deviation can be back-calculated $SD = SE(\sqrt{n})$ to 74.42. Based on these values and standard normal probability, the probability of being between 194.5 and 195.5 is 0.00896.

15. Rebecca A. Fox et al., "Behavioural Profile Predicts Dominance Status in Mountain Chickadees," *Animal Behaviour* 77, no. 6 (June 2009): 1441–48.

16. T. D. Williams, "Individual Variation in Endocrine Systems: Moving Beyond the 'Tyranny of the Golden Mean,'" *Philosophical Transactions of the Royal Society B: Biological Sciences* 363, no. 1497 (May 2008): 1687–98.

17. De Waal, *The Bonobo and the Atheist*.

18. Lee C. Drickamer and Stephen H. Vessey, *Animal Behavior: Concepts, Processes, and Methods* (Boston: PWS Publishers, 1986).

19. Temple Grandin and Catherine Johnson, *Animals in Translation: Using the Mysteries of Autism to Decode Animal Behavior* (Orlando, FL: Harcourt, 2006).

20. K. R. L. Hall and George B. Schaller, "Tool-Using Behavior of the California Sea Otter," *Journal of Mammalogy* 45, no. 2 (May 1964): 287–98.

21. Gema Martin-Ordas, Lena Schumacher, and Josep Call, "Sequential Tool Use in Great Apes," *PLoS ONE* 7, no. 12 (December 26, 2012); J. J. H. St. Clair and C. Rutz, "New Caledonian Crows Attend to Multiple Functional Properties of Complex Tools," *Philosophical Transactions of the Royal Society B: Biological Sciences* 368, no. 1630 (October 7, 2013): 20120415.

22. Michael Krützen et al., "Cultural Transmission of Tool Use in Bottlenose Dolphins," *Proceedings of the National Academy of Sciences of the United States of America* 102, no. 25 (2005): 8939–43.

23. Hélène Cochet and Richard W. Byrne, "Evolutionary Origins of Human Handedness: Evaluating Contrasting Hypotheses," *Animal Cognition* 16, no. 4 (July 2013): 531–42, doi:10.1007/s10071-013-0626-y.

24. William D. Hopkins et al., "Hand Preferences for Coordinated Bimanual Actions in 777 Great Apes: Implications for the Evolution of Handedness in Hominins," *Journal of Human Evolution* 60, no. 5 (May 2011): 605–11.

25. Miquel Llorente et al., "Population-Level Right-Handedness for a Coordinated Bimanual Task in Naturalistic Housed Chimpanzees: Replication and Extension in 114 Animals from Zambia and Spain," *American Journal of Primatology* 73, no. 3 (March 1, 2011): 281–90.

26. M. A. Hook and L. J. Rogers, "Development of Hand Preferences in Marmosets (*Callithrix jacchus*) and Effects of Aging," *Journal of Comparative Psychology* 114 (September 2000): 263–71.

27. Andrey Giljov et al., "Parallel Emergence of True Handedness in the Evolution of Marsupials and Placentals," *Current Biology* 25, no. 14 (July 2015): 1878–84.

28. Robert B. Found, "Ecological Implications of Personality in Elk," doctoral thesis, University of Alberta, 2015.

29. Christopher McDougall, "Natural Born Heroes," *RadioWest*, November 6, 2015, http://radiowest.kuer.org/post/natural-born-heroes-1.

30. Jennifer Bové, ed., *Back Road to Crazy: Stories from the Field* (Salt Lake City: University of Utah Press, 2005). Much of the account in this section is adapted from "Dances with Coyotes," a chapter I wrote for Bové.

31. Ibid.

32. Lori Schmidt, author interview, March 4, 2016.

33. Richard P. Thiel, Allison C. Thiel, and Marianne Strozewski, *Wild Wolves We Have Known: Stories of Wolf Biologists' Favorite Wolves* (Ely, MN: International Wolf Center, 2013).

34. Ibid.

35. Ibid., 204.

36. Kathryn Payne, William R. Langbauer Jr., and Elizabeth M. Thomas, "Infrasonic Calls of the Asian Elephant (*Elephas maximus*)," *Behavioral Ecology and Sociobiology* 18 (1986): 297–301.

37. Simon Gadbois and Catherine Reeve, "Canine Olfaction: Scent, Sign, and Situation," in *Domestic Dog Cognition and Behavior*, ed. Alexandra Horowitz (Berlin: Springer Berlin Heidelberg, 2014), 3–29.

38. Matthew Alice, "Dogs Can Smell Better Than People, but Exactly How Much Better?," *San Diego Reader*, November 15, 2001, http://www.sandiegoreader.com/news/2001/nov/15/dogs-can-smell-better-people-exactly-how-much-bett/.

39. L. J. McShane et al., "Repertoire, Structure, and Individual Variation of Vocalizations in the Sea Otter," *Journal of Mammalogy* 76, no. 2 (May 19, 1995): 414–27.

40. Payne, Langbauer, and Thomas, "Infrasonic Calls of the Asian Elephant (*Elephas maximus*)."

41. Patrick Bateson, "Assessment of Pain in Animals," *Animal Behviour* 42 (1991): 827–39.

CHAPTER 2: THE MYSTERY OF PERSONALITY

1. Stephen J. Suomi, Melinda A. Novak, and Arnold Well, "Aging in Rhesus Monkeys: Different Windows on Behavioral Continuity and Change," *Developmental Psychology* 32, no. 6 (1996): 1116–28.

2. Ibid., 1116.

3. Alecia J. Carter et al., "Animal Personality: What Are Behavioural Ecologists Measuring?," *Biological Reviews* 88, no. 2 (May 2013): 465–75.

4. "Overview of Personality Assessment," version 15, *Boundless*, May 26, 2016, https://www.boundless.com/psychology/textbooks/boundless-psychology-textbook/personality-16/assessing-personality-84/overview-of-personality-assessment-321-12856/.

5. C. G. Jung, *Psychological Types: Or, the Psychology of Individuation*, trans. H. Godwyn Baynes (New York: Harcourt, Brace, 1923).

6. Isobel Briggs Myers, Mary H. McCaulley, and Robert Most, *Manual: A Guide to the Development and Use of the Myers-Briggs Type Indicator* (orig. pub. 1962; Palo Alto, CA: Consulting Psychologists Press, 1985).

7. M. Drayton, "The Minnesota Multiphasic Personality Inventory-2 (MMPI-2)," *Occupational Medicine* 59, no. 2 (March 1, 2009): 135–36.

8. Samuel D. Gosling, Virginia S. Y. Kwan, and Oliver P. John, "A Dog's Got Personality: A Cross-Species Comparative Approach to Personality Judgments in Dogs and Humans," *Journal of Personality and Social Psychology* 85, no. 6 (2003): 1161–69.

9. "Personality Test Based on C. Jung and I. Briggs Myers Type Theory," Jung Typology Test, http://www.humanmetrics.com/cgi-win/jtypes2.asp.

10. "What Myers-Briggs Personality Type Was Adolf Hitler?," *Quora*, https://www.quora.com/What-Myers-Briggs-personality-type-was-Adolf-Hitler, accessed August 20, 2016.

11. Kenneth Libbrecht, *Ken Libbrecht's Field Guide to Snowflakes* (St. Paul: Voyageur Press, 2006).

12. Goodenough, McGuire, and Wallace, *Perspectives on Animal Behavior*.

13. Konrad Lorenz, "The Evolution of Behavior," *Scientific American* 199 (1958): 67–68.

14. Denise Cheung, author interview, March 25, 2016.

15. Walter G. Joyce, "The Origin of Turtles: A Paleontological Perspective," *Journal of Experimental Biology Part B: Molecular and Developmental Evolution* 324 (2015): 181–93.

CHAPTER 3: BRAVE FIGHTER OR SERENE LOVER

1. Paul R. Ehrlich, David S. Dobkin, and Darryl Wheye, *The Birder's Handbook: A Field Guide to the Natural History of North American Birds* (New York: Simon and Shuster, 1988).

2. R. A. Duckworth, "Aggressive Behaviour Affects Selection on Morphology by Influencing Settlement Patterns in a Passerine Bird," *Proceedings of the Royal Society B: Biological Sciences* 273, no. 1595 (July 22, 2006): 1789–95.

3. Ehrlich, Dobkin, and Wheye, *Birder's Handbook*.

4. Duckworth, "Aggressive Behaviour Affects Selection."

5. R. A. Duckworth, "Behavioral Correlations Across Breeding Contexts Provide a Mechanism for a Cost of Aggression," *Behavioral Ecology* 17, no. 6 (November 1, 2006): 1011–19.

6. Renée Duckworth, author interview, October 15, 2016.

7. Fox et al., "Behavioural Profile Predicts Dominance Status in Mountain Chickadees."

8. Kapil K. Khadka and Matthias W. Foellmer, "Does Personality Explain Variation in the Probability of Sexual Cannibalism in the Orb-Web Spider *Argiope aurantia*?," *Behaviour* 150, no. 14 (January 1, 2013): 1731–46.

9. Aric W. Berning et al., "Sexual Cannibalism Is Associated with Female Behavioural Type, Hunger State and Increased Hatching Success," *Animal Behaviour* 84, no. 3 (September 2012): 715–21.

10. Ibid., 719.

11. Göran Arnqvist and Stefan Henriksson, "Sexual Cannibalism in the Fishing Spider and a Model for the Evolution of Sexual Cannibalism Based on Genetic Constraints," *Evolutionary Ecology* 11, no. 3 (May 1997): 255–73.

12. David L. Hu, Brian Chan, and John W. M. Bush, "The Hydrodynamics of Water Strider Locomotion," *Nature* 424 (2003): 663–66.

13. Andrew Sih and Jason V. Watters, "The Mix Matters: Behavioural Types and Group Dynamics in Water Striders," *Behaviour* 142, no. 9–10 (2005): 1417–31.

14. Göran Arnqvist, "Pre-Copulatory Fighting in a Water Strider: Inter-Sexual Conflict or Mate Assessment?," *Animal Behaviour* 43 (1992): 559–67.

15. K. Okada et al., "Sexual Conflict over Mating in *Gnatocerus Cornutus*? Females Prefer Lovers Not Fighters," *Proceedings of the Royal Society B: Biological Sciences* 281, no. 1785 (May 7, 2014).

16. Ibid.

17. Stephanie S. Godfrey et al., "Lovers and Fighters in Sleepy Lizard Land: Where Do Aggressive Males Fit in a Social Network?," *Animal Behaviour* 83, no. 1 (January 2012): 209–15.

18. Ibid.

19. "*This Is Spinal Tap*," *Wikipedia* entry, https://en.wikipedia.org/w/index.php?title=This_Is_Spinal_Tap&oldid=738165828, accessed September 7, 2016.

CHAPTER 4: APPETITE OR APPETIZER

1. Robert M. Timm et al., "Coyote Attacks: An Increasing Suburban Problem," paper, 69th North American Wildlife and Natural Resources Conference, Spokane, WA, 2004.

2. John A. Shivik, *The Predator Paradox: Ending the War with Wolves, Bears, Cougars, and Coyotes* (Boston: Beacon Press, 2014).

3. Gordon Grice, *Deadly Kingdom: The Book of Dangerous Animals* (New York: Dial Press, 2010).

4. Mark E. McNay, "A Case History of Wolf-Human Encounters in Alaska and Canada," *Alaska Department of Fish and Game Technical Bulletin* 13 (2002).

5. Marco Musiani and Elisabetta Visalberghi, "Effectiveness of Fladry on Wolves in Captivity," *Wildlife Society Bulletin* 29, no. 1 (April 1, 2001): 91–98.

6. Nathan Lance, "Application of Electrified Fladry to Decrease Risk of Livestock Depredations by Wolves (*Canis lupus*)," master's thesis, Utah State University, 2009.

7. Patrick Myers, author interview, August 19, 2016.

8. Donald W. Meyers, "Utah Family Wants Bear Alert in Dead Son's Name," *Salt Lake Tribune*, May 4, 2011, http://archive.sltrib.com/story.php?ref= /sltrib/news/51750448-78/bear-ives-family-sam.html.csp.

9. "Girl, 12, Thought She Was a 'Goner' in Bear Attack," *ABC News*, August 20, 2013, http://abcnews.go.com/US/12-year-girl-thought-goner-bear-attack/story?id=19997134.

10. Stephen Herrero, *Bear Attacks: Their Causes and Avoidance* (orig. pub. 1985; Guilford, CT: Lyons Press, 2002); Stephen Herrero et al., "Fatal Attacks by American Black Bear on People: 1900–2009," *Journal of Wildlife Management* 75, no. 3 (2011): 596–603.

11. Myers, author interview.

12. Cristina Eisenberg, *The Wolf's Tooth: Keystone Predators, Trophic Cascades, and Biodiversity* (Washington, DC: Island Press, 2011); William Stolzenburg, *Where the Wild Things Were: Life, Death, and Ecological Wreckage in a Land of Vanishing Predators* (New York: Bloomsbury, 2008).

13. Joel Berger, *The Better to Eat You With: Fear in the Animal World* (Chicago: University of Chicago Press, 2008).

14. William J. Ripple and Robert L. Beschta, "Wolves and the Ecology of Fear: Can Predation Risk Structure Ecosystems?," *BioScience* 54, no. 8 (2004): 755.

15. Berger, *The Better to Eat You With*.

16. "Do Animals Have Personality? The Importance of Individual Differences," *BioScience* 62, no. 6 (June 2012): 533–37.

17. Found, "Ecological Implications of Personality in Elk."

18. Lynne Gilbert-Norton, author interview, October 7, 2016.

19. Laurel Braitman, *Animal Madness: Inside Their Minds* (orig. pub. 2014; New York: Simon & Schuster, 2015).

20. J. Chadwick Johnson and Andrew Sih, "Fear, Food, Sex and Parental Care: A Syndrome of Boldness in the Fishing Spider, *Dolomedes triton*," *Animal Behaviour* 74, no. 5 (November 2007): 1131–38.

21. L. T. Reaney and P. R.Y. Backwell, "Risk-Taking Behavior Predicts Aggression and Mating Success in a Fiddler Crab," *Behavioral Ecology* 18, no. 3 (March 30, 2007): 521–25.

22. Claudio Carere and Dario Maestripieri, *Animal Personalities: Behavior, Physiology, and Evolution* (Chicago: University of Chicago Press, 2013).

23. J. L. Quinn, E. F. Cole, J. Bates, R. W. Payne, and W. Cresswell, "Personality Predicts Individual Responsiveness to the Risks of Starvation and Predation," *Proceedings of the Royal Society B* 279 (2012): 1919–26.

24. Andrew Sih, Lee B. Kats, and Eric F. Maurer, "Behavioural Correlations Across Situations and the Evolution of Antipredator Behaviour in a Sunfish-Salamander System," *Animal Behaviour* 65, no. 1 (January 2003): 29–44.

25. Andrew Sih and Lee B. Kats, "Age, Experience, and the Response of Streamside Salamander Hatchlings to Chemical Cues from Predatory Sunfish," *Ethology* 96, no. 3 (January 12, 1994): 253–59, doi:10.1111/j.1439–0310.1994.tb01013.x.

26. Sih, Kats, and Maurer, "Behavioural Correlations Across Situations and the Evolution of Antipredator Behaviour in a Sunfish-Salamander System."

27. Ibid.

CHAPTER 5: HERD OR HERMIT

1. Elizabeth Liverman, author interview, June 18, 2016.

2. *Touched by a Horse*, http://www.touchedbyahorse.com/.

3. Susan Riechert and Thomas Jones, "Phenotypic Variation in the Social Behaviour of the Spider *Anelosimus studiosus* Along a Latitudinal Gradient," *Animal Behaviour* 75, no. 6 (June 2008): 1893–1902. From Riechert and Jones, I used the data in table 1 to perform a simple correlation between latitude and maximum number of females. The resulting coefficient of determination (r^2, which indicates how well the model fit the data) was 0.71, thus indicating that 71 percent of the variation in the number of females in a nest was explained by the latitude where the nest was built.

4. Ibid.

5. Uta Seibt and Wolfgang Wickler, "Why Do 'Family Spiders,' *Stegodyphus (Eresidae)*, Live in Colonies?," *Journal of Arachnology* (1988): 193–98.

6. Thomas C. Jones et al., "Fostering Model Explains Variation in Levels of Sociality in a Spider System," *Animal Behaviour* 73, no. 1 (January 2007): 195–204.

7. Godfrey et al., "Lovers and Fighters in Sleepy Lizard Land."

8. Culum Brown and Eleanor Irving, "Individual Personality Traits Influence Group Exploration in a Feral Guppy Population," *Behavioral Ecology* 25, no. 1 (October 3, 2013).

9. Shermin de Silva, Ashoka D. G. Ranjeewa, and Sergey Kryazhimskiy, "The Dynamics of Social Networks Among Female Asian Elephants," *BMC Ecology* 11, no. 17 (July 27, 2012).

10. David Lusseau et al., "Quantifying the Influence of Sociality on Population Structure in Bottlenose Dolphins," *Journal of Animal Ecology* 75, no. 1 (January 2006): 14–24.

11. Ibid., 19.

12. G. Kerth, N. Perony, and F. Schweitzer, "Bats Are Able to Maintain Long-Term Social Relationships Despite the High Fission-Fusion Dynamics of Their Groups," *Proceedings of the Royal Society B: Biological Sciences* 278, no. 1719 (September 22, 2011).

13. David Stoner, author interview, June 10, 2016.

14. Bernd Heinrich, *Mind of the Raven: Investigations and Adventures with Wolf-Birds* (orig. pub. 1999; New York: Harper Perennial, 2007).

CHAPTER 6: WAYFARER OR WALLFLOWER

1. Else J. Fjerdingstad et al., "Evolution of Dispersal and Life History Strategies—*Tetrahymena* ciliates," *BMC Evolutionary Biology* 7, no. 1 (2007): 133.
2. Julien Cote et al., "Personality-Dependent Dispersal: Characterization, Ontogeny and Consequences for Spatially Structured Populations," *Philosophical Transactions of the Royal Society B: Biological Sciences* 365, no. 1560 (December 27, 2010): 4065–76.
3. Julien Cote et al., "Personality Traits and Dispersal Tendency in the Invasive Mosquitofish (*Gambusia affinis*)," *Proceedings of the Royal Society B: Biological Sciences* 277, no. 1687 (May 22, 2010): 1571–79.
4. Renée A. Duckworth, Virginia Belloni, and Samantha R. Anderson, "Cycles of Species Replacement Emerge from Locally Induced Maternal Effects on Offspring Behavior in a Passerine Bird," *Science* 347, no. 6224 (2015): 875–77.
5. Ibid.
6. Duckworth, "Behavioral Correlations Across Breeding Contexts."
7. Ibid.
8. Renée A. Duckworth, "Adaptive Dispersal Strategies and the Dynamics of a Range Expansion," *American Naturalist* 172, supplement (July 2008): S4–S17.
9. Christiaan Both et al., "Pairs of Extreme Avian Personalities Have Highest Reproductive Success," *Journal of Animal Ecology* 74, no. 4 (2005): 667–74.

CHAPTER 7: NATURE AND NURTURE

1. Niels J. Dingemanse et al., "Natal Dispersal and Personalities in Great Tits (*Parus Major*)," *Proceedings of the Royal Society of London B: Biological Sciences* 270, no. 1516 (2003): 741–47.
2. Pieter J. Drent, Kees van Oers, and Arie J. van Noordwijk, "Realized Heritability of Personalities in the Great Tit (*Parus Major*)," *Proceedings of the Royal Society of London B: Biological Sciences* 270, no. 1510 (2003): 45–51.
3. Kayla Sweeney et al., "Assessing the Effects of Rearing Environment, Natural Selection, and Developmental Stage on the Emergence of a Behavioral Syndrome," *Ethology* 119, no. 5 (May 2013): 436–47.
4. Ibid., 445.
5. Theodosius Dobzhansky, "Nothing in Biology Makes Sense Except in the Light of Evolution," *American Biology Teacher* 35, no. 3 (March 1973): 125–29.
6. Richard Dawkins, *The Selfish Gene*, 30th anniv. ed. (Oxford, UK: Oxford University Press, 2006).
7. Claudio Carere et al., "Personalities in Great Tits, *Parus Major*: Stability and Consistency," *Animal Behaviour* 70, no. 4 (October 2005): 795–805.
8. Lucy Jones, "A Soviet Scientist Created the Only Tame Foxes in the World," BBC, http://www.bbc.com/earth/story/20160912-a-soviet-scientist -created-the-only-tame-foxes-in-the-world, accessed October 2, 2016.

9. Lyudmila Trut, Irina Oskina, and Anastasiya Kharlamova, "Animal Evolution During Domestication: The Domesticated Fox as a Model," *BioEssays* 31, no. 3 (March 2009): 349–60.

10. "Fox in a Box—The New Pet Craze," *Russia Today*, http://newsvideo.su /video/1727075, accessed May 28, 2017.

11. Raymond Coppinger and Lorna Coppinger, *Dogs: A New Understanding of Canine Origin, Behavior and Evolution* (Chicago: University of Chicago Press, 2002).

12. N. J. Dingemanse et al., "Fitness Consequences of Avian Personalities in a Fluctuating Environment," *Proceedings of the Royal Society B: Biological Sciences* 271, no. 1541 (April 22, 2004): 847–52.

13. Niels J. Dingemanse and Denis Réale, "Natural Selection and Animal Personality," *Behaviour* 142, no. 9–10 (2005): 1159–1184.

14. Denis Réale et al., "Consistency of Temperament in Bighorn Ewes and Correlates with Behaviour and Life History," *Animal Behaviour* 60, no. 5 (November 2000): 589–97.

15. J. M. Lusher, C. Chandler, and D. Ball, "Dopamine D4 Receptor Gene (DRD4) Is Associated with Novelty Seeking (NS) and Substance Abuse: The Saga Continues . . . ," *Molecular Psychiatry* 6, no. 5 (September 2001): 497–99.

16. Peter Korsten et al., "Association Between DRD4 Gene Polymorphism and Personality Variation in Great Tits: A Test Across Four Wild Populations," *Molecular Ecology* 19, no. 4 (February 2010): 832–43.

17. Braitman, *Animal Madness*.

18. Shau-Kwaun Chen et al., "Hematopoietic Origin of Pathological Grooming in Hoxb8 Mutant Mice," *Cell* 141, no. 5 (May 2010): 775–85.

19. Duckworth, author interview.

20. Tessa Roseboom, Susanne de Rooij, and Rebecca Painter, "The Dutch Famine and Its Long-Term Consequences for Adult Health," *Early Human Development* 82, no. 8 (August 2006): 485–91.

CHAPTER 8: THE SELFISH HERD, THE GENEROUS GENE

1. R. W. Fairfull, L. McMillan, and W. M. Muir, "Poultry Breeding: Progress and Prospects for Genetic Improvement of Egg and Meat Production," Centre for Genetic Improvement of Livestock, University of Guelph, Ontario, http://cgil.uoguelph.ca/pub/6wcgalp/6wcFairfull.pdf, accessed October 10, 2016.

2. Margaret Heffernan, "Is the Professional Pecking Order Doing More Harm Than Good?," TED Talk, October 2, 2015, http://www.npr.org /2015/10/02/443412777/is-the-professional-pecking-order-doing-more -harm-than-good.

3. W. M. Muir and J. V. Craig, "Improving Animal Well-Being Through Genetic Selection," *Poultry Science* 77, no. 12 (1998): 1781–88.

4. Stefan Riedel, "Edward Jenner and the History of Smallpox and Vaccination," *Baylor University Medical Center Proceedings* 18 (January 2005): 21, http://search.proquest.com/openview/85ba45308e9fd96b6db64f63fcf6d882.

5. "Variables: The Story of Smallpox—and Other Deadly Eurasian Germs," *Gun, Germs, and Steel*, PBS, http://www.pbs.org/gunsgermssteel/variables/smallpox.html, accessed July 2, 2016.

6. John Novembre, Alison P. Galvani, and Montgomery Slarkin, "The Geographic Spread of the CCR5 Δ32 HIV-Resistance Allele," *PLOS Biology* 3, no. 11 (2005): 1954–62.

7. Dawkins, *The Selfish Gene*.

8. Jamie Strange, author interview, March 4, 2016.

9. "Honey Bee Disorders: Honey Bee Parasites," Honey Bee Program, University of Georgia, http://www.ent.uga.edu/bees/disorders/honey-bee-parasites.html, accessed October 8, 2016.

10. J. P. Strange, "Nest Initiation in Three North American Bumble Bees (*Bombus*): Gyne Number and Presence of Honey Bee Workers Influence Establishment Success and Colony Size," *Journal of Insect Science* 10, no. 1 (2010): 1–11.

11. James Surowiecki, *The Wisdom of Crowds: Why the Many Are Smarter Than the Few* (New York: Anchor, 2005).

12. De Waal, *The Bonobo and the Atheist*.

CHAPTER 9: PAIRING SINGULARITIES

1. "If by Chance We Meet Again," *This American Life*, http://www.this americanlife.org/radio-archives/episode/291/reunited-and-it-feels-so -good?act=2, accessed September 16, 2016.

2. Wayne Pacelle, *The Bond: Our Kinship with Animals, Our Call to Defend Them* (orig. pub. 2011; New York: William Morrow Paperbacks, 2012).

3. F. Aureli and C. M. Schaffner, "Aggression and Conflict Management at Fusion in Spider Monkeys," *Biology Letters* 2007, no. 3 (2007): 147–49.

4. Ibid., 147.

5. De Waal, *The Bonobo and the Atheist*.

6. Gilbert-Norton, author interview.

7. "Canines with a Cause—Saving Three Lives," https://canineswithacause .org/, accessed October 16, 2016.

8. Fink et al., "Men's Personality and Women's Perception of Their Dance Quality," *Personality and Individual Differences* 52 (January 2012): 232–35.

9. Safina, *Beyond Words*.

10. Edward O. Wilson, *Biophilia* (Cambridge, MA: Harvard University Press, 1984).

11. Stoner, author interview.

Index